"*40 Days with Grace* is a gem. Not only a reminder but reassurance that God is always there to lean on during our toughest of times. Plunging down into any 'Hole' can be terrifying. But not only was Yahweh Sherylle's strength and light in the darkness, but in showing His incredible awesomeness and immense love for her, He transformed that hole into something beautiful. What a gift! Sherylle's faith inspires me to delve deeper into God's Word as I move through my own life struggles. Knowing that we are not alone is the biggest blessing of all and is what I cling to when things get really tough. God is there to take our hand as we walk without fear in whatever we are facing in life.

—SUSAN ROWE | Primary School Teacher, Qld

"What a beautiful devotional. This book has really touched my heart and soul. While I have not lived Sherylle' s life, there are so many parts of this book that I feel were written for me. Thank you so much! The lessons, the Word, the humour, the easy-to-understand analogies, the real-life stories, the trials and tribulations, the many ups, the positives, the 'light at the end of the tunnel', the beautiful moments, and the sad – it has everything. There is something in *40 Days with Grace* for everyone.

—LAURA GRAF | Primary School Teacher, Qld

40 Days With Grace

A daily walk with Jesus into peace, joy and healing

SHERYLLE GRACE WELLS

Ark House Press
arkhousepress.com

© 2021 Sherylle Grace Wells

All rights reserved. Apart from any fair dealing for the purpose of study, research, criticism, or review, as permitted under the Copyright Act, no part may be reproduced by any process without written permission.

Unless otherwise stated, all Scriptures are taken from the New International Translation (Holy Bible. Copyright© 1996, 2004, 2007, 2013 by Tyndale House Foundation. Used by permission of Tyndale House Publishers Inc., Carol Stream, Illinois 60188. All rights reserved.)

Some names and identifying details have been changed to protect the privacy of individuals.

Cataloguing in Publication Data:
Title: 40 Days With Grace
ISBN: 978-0-6453220-1-9 (pbk)
Subjects: Devotional;
Other Authors/Contributors: Wells, Sherylle Grace

Design by initiateagency.com
Editor: Wendy Stuart, www.wendyandwords.com
Bible verses are from the Bible in the Public Domain: World English Bible (WEB)

Dedicated to my family
Robin
Danielle, Joel & Stephannie
who have travelled with me on this journey.
But mostly to Jesus, my Saviour, who has always been with me, preparing the way.
I thank you all.
You are my treasure.

Contents

How Great xi
Introduction xiii
The Hole xix
Chapter 1   Look Around 1
Chapter 2   Sometimes 3
Chapter 3   Jewels 5
Chapter 4   Come Home 7
Chapter 5   Thoughts 9
Chapter 6   Overall Design 11
Chapter 7   Vision 13
Chapter 8   God-Shocked 15
Chapter 9   Baking 17
    Pavlova 19
Chapter 10 Washing Up 20
Chapter 11 Ice Cream 22
Chapter 12 Daffodils 24
Chapter 13 Succulent Delight 26
Chapter 14 Prickles 28
Chapter 15 Surprise Attack! 30
Chapter 16 Impossible Forgiveness 33
Chapter 17 Heights 35
Chapter 18 Deliverance 37
Chapter 19 Hidden Blessings 39

Chapter 20	Detour	41
	Just Trust	43
Chapter 21	Timely Rescue	44
Chapter 22	Midnight Awakening	46
Chapter 23	Sequence Of Events	49
Chapter 24	Christian Ducks	51
Chapter 25	The Lazy Sheepdog	53
Chapter 26	Sculptures	55
Chapter 27	Insignificant	58
Chapter 28	Implanted	60
Chapter 29	The Chair	62
Chapter 30	Terrible Loss	64
Chapter 31	Sticks And Stones	66
Chapter 32	PTSD	68
	It Rained Today	70
Chapter 33	Grandma's Prayers	71
Chapter 34	Our Children	73
Chapter 35	A Parent's Heart	75
Chapter 36	For A Hurting Friend	77
Chapter 37	Big Arms	79
Chapter 38	Realising A Dream	81
Chapter 39	You Are Invited	83
Chapter 40	Riding The Waves	85
	Salvation Prayer	87
Resources And Help		89
About The Author		91

How Great

How great would it be if Jesus would come
To sit at my table and feast on some.
To share in a meal of delicious food,
I'd savour and taste on His every word.

My appetite for more would definitely increase.
Problems around me would certainly cease!
To know and to feel His Divine Presence
would be to me of great excellence!

But for me now, I sit and I wait,
I devour His Word and I meditate.
Opening up my old Bible reveals words of truth,
and I know in my heart that it happens by faith.

So I keep on devouring GOD's words for me.
I see new insights that inspire perfectly.
His words touch me deeply, Holy Spirit inspired
And I know by faith, He's here the whole time!

Sherylle Grace Wells

Introduction

Are you busy? Needing some quiet? Some answers? Maybe just some rest in the Lord to heal. This book is your invitation to take some time out and sit quietly with GOD for a while each day. To be still. The Hebrew word for 'be still' means to 'let go, to release'. To surrender. There's so much we want to let go of to be with GOD and know Him. We want to let go of our pains, our traumas and anything obscuring our experience of GOD and the peace and joy He offers. A great starting point can be a simple daily practice of sitting in His Grace through prayer and His Word, and through hearing how others have done the same to know GOD, to heal and to grow.

I've written this book to feel like we are sitting around the breakfast table every morning, sisters in Christ. I will encourage you to read GOD's word, the Bible, hear some meaningful stories and insights, and then pray and reflect. May these times be enriching, healing and freeing.

There will be a special guest, always. He's never late, and He loves your company. GOD wants to meet with you. Yes! GOD will be there.

You see, my experience is that GOD is never far away. It is only us who move away. He holds us firmly but lovingly. We just need to hold firmly back! A daily devotional is a way to seal your commitment with Him every day. It is also, as you will find in my story, a strategic key to dealing with all that life throws at you – or GOD trusts you with.

Within the 40 devotionals I share my own stories and personal experiences – some 'good' experiences and some 'not so good' – well, let's say 'painful'. There's a lot to be said for the power of story to move us, connect us and open our imagination to possibilities. Don't worry. My stories have happy endings.

I also share my reflections, learnings and prayers that brought me to experience GOD's grace first-hand even in the toughest of times – times that included cancer, betrayal, grief from loss, divorce and family trauma. My experience is that GOD can make good out of *every* experience we go through. It's a cliché but true: He is the champion of making lemonade out of lemons. So essentially, this is a book of hope.

From A 'Hole' To 'Whole'

Perhaps like me you've had a few servings of lemons in life. My children and I were served up one great big sour lemon of abuse, betrayal and trauma that shook our world and took us down a dark 'hole'. This book begins with 'The Hole', which is a short rendition of that time. Perhaps you will recognise your story in ours.

After we emerged from those experiences, by the Grace of GOD, I could reflect and see how every step of the way He had provided for us. Key to receiving this support was my time desperately searching the scriptures for guidance and sustenance, where GOD imprinted His thoughts into my mind and heart. Many of these are shared with you in these 40 days of devotions. In fact, it was in my times spent with GOD in that 'hole' that I became more sensitive to His leading and His quiet Holy Spirit voice. He ultimately helped me face the biggest battle of all – finding forgiveness for those who had hurt me and my children, leaving bitterness behind.

Yes, it is possible to forgive, and therein lies true freedom.

I write now as an older, wiser woman who is encouraging you to get into the habit of regularly spending time with Jesus and drawing strength from Him for what lies ahead. I hope you will appreciate the lesson of blessing I received from each experience and that insights gained will draw you closer to your Heavenly Father.

While I wrote this book and looked back at my life, GOD reminded me of memories and feelings long since subsided. He would provide a thought, and as I started to write, more words would naturally flow, guided by the Holy Spirit. I was given fresh understandings of how He had helped me through those times and the lessons learned.

GOD meets you wherever you are. My inspiration for my poem *It Rained Today* actually came while taking a shower! You too will find that through your daily practice, you will recognise the voice of the Holy Spirit more keenly.

How To Read This Book

This book is designed to be read daily for 40 days. But we are all individuals, so you can choose to read one each day or each week. It's up to you. I recommend daily as I know how much that helped me.

As you begin to read each devotional, savour the words of GOD first in your Bible, then spend some time contemplating their meaning. The Holy Spirit is gentle, and He will speak into your mind. Then read the story and lastly pray. As you go into your day, think about what you have read and journal your thoughts. It will prove interesting as you look back. I pray that these stories will engender a strong hunger within to learn more of GOD's character as you read the Bible and contemplate.

Why 40 days? Well, that's GOD's concept found in the Bible. For example, Jesus fasted for 40 days and nights in the Judean wilderness. There were 40 days between Jesus' resurrection and ascension, and who can forget the great flood. Forty days is simply a period in which we allow GOD to do His work in us as we set our minds on Him. He set it; let's do it together.

Why 'grace'? While Grace is my maiden name, the grace here is much more than that. Someone has said that it's an acronym: GOD's Riches at Christ's Expense. In Psalm 145:8 we read that the Lord is compassionate, slow to anger, and abounding in love and faithfulness. He is gracious and He gives grace, His unearned favour. That's who He is. And His love and mercy naturally extend from that grace. They are inseparable. Your devotional time is your invitation for your Heavenly Father to come.

You will notice I always write GOD's name in all capitals. Afterall, GOD is the Creator, holy, righteous and magnificent in His power. He is the origin of love who lives forever. He is love! (1 John 4:16) Only man-made powerless gods crafted by humans get their names written in lower case. Not our mighty GOD. Another name for GOD I use is 'Yahweh', the ancient Hebrew name.

Reach for His grace during these 40 days, and beyond. The fruits of grace are love, joy, peace and forgiveness. Transformation will occur as we are moulded into His likeness more and more. As you receive His grace, learn to walk in it and view other people in the light of His love for them. His grace is undeserved but freely given.

May your relationship with our Heavenly Father become deeper and closer as you journey with His Grace to peace, joy and true freedom.

Remember, there is no sin or pain too great for our GOD to heal or forgive. GOD is healer and may He touch and heal your life as He has mine.

You shall call on me, and you shall go and pray to me, and I will listen to you. You shall seek me, and find me, when you search for me with all your heart.

Jeremiah 29:12–13

The Hole

Our Story

On a glorious day in May 1990, our family picnicked with friends at a local park, having a most wonderful time. The next day was the opposite.

My husband came home from night shift angry and disillusioned. He had failed his second attempt at his paramedic exam and now was unable to be promoted. Harmony was shot, but I quietly pursued my lunch-making duties and took the kids to school. One had recently begun Year One and the other was in Year Four. I came home to a conversation over coffee that started with him asking, 'Why did GOD let me down?' Before I could offer any response, he stated that he didn't think he loved me and took off to visit a friend of his, a woman whom I had felt quite alarmed about.

Holding back tears, I went to work but felt sick and could not eat. Meanwhile he removed some of his possessions from our home. That was the beginning of the end of our almost 15-year marriage. It was over in one day. What? I was shocked and devastated. I thought I had married for life.

The following weekend was heart wrenching as I explained the situation to our children, then to my family and then to his mother – on Mothers' Day. It was difficult for all of us. He made it clear that it was final and there was no going back. I found out on the 'grapevine' that he had been making fun of me and laughing. As he drove up the driveway for the last time, to collect more things, disappointment and anguish flooded my spirit. These emotions remained for days. I felt worthless. His leaving was the biggest kick in the teeth ever, with even greater pain than the first time he had been unfaithful.

My son became so distressed that he said he wanted to fall on the road under a truck, so I desperately rang Lifeline. After listening to my story, a caring counsellor explained to us that we had been through a huge shock. Our world had been violently shaken like an earthquake, and there would still be some aftershocks for a while. She told us that connections in our lives would now change, and we would be facing a 'hole', which we all would have to go down into. But she reassured us we would eventually rise again.

I dealt with this 'hole' at first by pretending that it wasn't there. No way was I was going to go through a hole! I was starting to feel stronger and decided that I would be fine. My plan was to support my children all the way through their 'hole' experiences.

But before long there it was, in front of me. Still, I didn't acknowledge it. I kept on going and continued denying that I was approaching a huge pit of unfamiliar territory full of emotions I wanted to avoid. Finally, I couldn't ignore those tumultuous emotions inside any longer. As I reluctantly and steadily stepped down into the dark, seemingly bottomless pit, I allowed myself to become awash with those new emotions. And thus began a step-by-step journey.

For a day or two I would allow myself to wallow in depression and misery. To really feel it. Some days my depression was a heavy weight on my chest. I would desperately cry out, 'Jesus!' and He would rescue me. I would find myself landing on a safe 'ledge'. Something to rest on! A respite from the emotional turmoil.

The First Ledge

The first ledge was a temporary home with my sister Del and her family after I had sold my house, by the grace of GOD, in only two weeks. They graciously let us stay with them. The three of us moved into the rumpus room, which, being in my positive state of mind, I renamed the 'Aunty Flat'. This became our home for the next three months. There on this ledge of safety I was strengthened by supportive family and encouraging friends. My children and I really needed that. GOD knew. He had provided.

My young children were attending a supportive school and were receiving great care and understanding from the staff. So they remained at that school, and we stayed in our own church for some stability.

Life was tricky and interactions with my ex-husband and his new lady were difficult. I was totally out of my comfort zone and now making decisions that I'd never had to contemplate before. I still felt my life was tumbling downwards, but I chose to keep our morale up with as much normality and positivity as I could muster.

My sister advised me to look after my exterior, so I wore make-up and high heels every day, which helped my self-esteem. Because I could sew well, I made all our clothes and we looked pretty spiffy, although on the inside I sometimes felt like jelly. Positive feedback about how we looked and how we were doing was encouraging, and like riding a bicycle, I kept balancing. The wheels kept turning... As I felt better about myself it showed, and because of that, I kept cycling.

Quietly, I was trusting GOD and getting to know Him better and trying not to become bitter. When the time was right, I would begin to descend further in the pit, enduring a fresh bout of grief and fear of the unknown. It was scary... Then I would find myself involuntarily stepping down onto another ledge. Whew! It was getting darker, but I found special Bible verses that illuminated the way, guiding my downward pathway as I desperately clung to yet another ledge.

In those times I would frantically reach out to GOD, searching the Bible and discovering that its pages were becoming alive as I found

His special promises. The verses jumped right out of the pages to me. GOD was talking to me. I'd been reading the Bible since my conversion at 15, but now I was delving deeper, desperate for guidance. His promises strengthened my faith.

During one of these times, I finally took off my wedding ring. It felt dirty and symbolised a loveless marriage, now defunct. I took off the dead ring but felt uncomfortable with wearing no ring. So Del took me shopping and I bought an 'S'-shaped ring with a tiny diamond. The 'S' stood for Sherylle, but soon it also meant 'special' because I was feeling special to GOD. On reflection, perhaps it also meant 'strong'.

I felt ready to step out again off my safe ledge. The bottom was still not in sight, and I understood that it was necessary to step out, armed with my sword, the Word of GOD. (Ephesians 6:17). Eventually I realised that those solid ledges were my faith in substance. A strong faith in my rock-solid GOD who was sustaining me. Discovering my faith to be real and actual was astounding! GOD had developed and changed me into a stronger person as He stretched me, and I put into practice what I read in His Word. Jesus said that if we have faith the size of a mustard seed, it can move a mountain. I found that to be completely true!

Going deeper and deeper into the hole and into my faith, I was no longer afraid because a new confidence in my Lord was growing inside me. He was nourishing and sustaining me all along my downward trek. My new journey was beginning to get more interesting and slightly exciting.

After financial separation, and with the help of a loan, I bought a little car and a small house. I did what we needed in connecting electricity, gas and so on after we moved in. After that, I had $13 in the bank. Praise GOD – I'd been given sufficient for my needs! That had to be the work of my perfect, organised Heavenly Father!

More Rumbles And Tumbles

Things were beginning to settle down a bit. Perhaps the end was nigh! Then, without warning, those earthquake rumbles were back!

After school one day, my daughter came down the hallway, wringing her hands and saying she had to talk to me.

'Um.... Mum ... while Daddy was with us, he did things to me.' Her eyes dropped to the floor.

'What? What things?' My stomach lurched yet I gently lifted her chin.

She then told me he'd touched her sexually, explaining in detail things he'd done. I was shocked and sickened. This news hit me like a bus. It was completely out of the blue. I knew she had told me she was relieved when he left, but I hadn't picked up on any of this. How could I have missed this?!! She'd given no indications. Or did I miss them?

I learned that she was bringing forth this information now as I had been served divorce papers and she believed he was divorcing all of us. She felt this an opportunity to 'tell on him' and be safe.

I wrapped my arms around her, and we wept together. My heart broke, and I could feel myself going down into the treacherous depths again. This time, I tumbled, and my daughter with me. Will this pit ever have a bottom?

Shock, horror and strangely relief flooded my being. Shocked because I thought I had always protected her and her brother, horrified because this was abhorrent, and relieved because I would no longer have to send them for weekend visits with their father. I had never felt comfortable with these access visits.

I immediately rang the guidance centre my son and daughter attended for counselling and reported the disclosure. Police came to visit within a few days. There were interviews, recordings and enough evidence for charges to be laid, with access to the children by their father denied. It went to court – first the Magistrates Court and then up to District Court.

After two years, we finally had our day in the District Court. I went into that courtroom feeling prepared and safe despite everything shaking around me because I held tightly to GOD's special promises from His Word. Two verses from the Book of Psalms and two songs – *Be bold, be strong for the Lord your GOD is with you* and *My GOD is an awesome GOD* – strengthened me for the days ahead in court. I felt like Moses as the Israelites fought against their enemies. When Aaron and Hur supported Moses' arms, the battle was won. These two verses and two songs held up my spiritual arms and, yes, our battle was won. My ex-husband was convicted on all counts against him. Justice was served.

The rumblings of our earthquake stopped, and I felt stronger than ever. My daughter and son were gaining strength through counselling and family comfort. We had endured and survived. I went on singing songs of praise.

While the external battle had been won, however, there was still one final battle going on inside me. I had to forgive my ex-husband for everything he had done – all the upheavals, the sexual abuse, the rejection and all the pain. I tried to forgive him because it was what was required of me for my relationship with my Heavenly Father to continue harmoniously. But it seemed impossible.

Then GOD once again stepped into my darkness. It was a Sunday night, after a Christian singles camp on Forgiveness. I felt convicted to release my unforgiveness. My loving Father could see my hurting heart and my obedience to do His will. He showed me a vision of His hand reaching out. I knew that if I put my hand into His, forgiveness would occur. I knew I had to take His offer. As I did so, forgiveness flooded my soul. Something that I couldn't do, He did!

The excruciating pain that had been crushing my heart was now obliterated. And now I could heal. I was free!

I was finally emerging from the hole awash with relief and gladness at having triumphed. Looking back on the hole, I saw that it was beautiful! I realised that while I had stopped on those ledges, I had planted seeds on each one. These had grown into beautiful flowers and fruit cascading down the slopes, and GOD's powerful light was illuminating the new valley.

The seeds were seeds from promises, seeds of teaching, seeds of testimonies and learning, times with family and friends, growing times. I had met special friends through my tears, joy and laughter, who were fertilizer for the seeds to grow. The ugly, terrifying hole had been transformed into something utterly gorgeous and I was amazed at the outstanding beauty of the providential fruit.

Gratitude For The Whole Experience

I now had a strong testimony of GOD's extreme goodness in the face of terrible adversity and sadness. I was stronger, and this continues as I trust in GOD who has never failed me and never will! I look back at that wilderness experience with joy as I see strong evidence of His sustaining power to overcome all possible horrors, past, present and into the future. My faith has been deepened and I can say wholeheartedly that the experience was utterly worthwhile, although I never would have chosen it.

The hole which I denied at first, I now proudly own and am grateful to GOD for leading me and my children through. I can confidently say that whatever He does is good, whether we see that or not. He works everything for our good. I thank Him for the 'whole' experience and for walking with Grace with me.

1

Look Around

> Praise Yahweh from the earth, you great sea creatures, and all depths; lightning and hail, snow and clouds; stormy wind, fulfilling his word; mountains and all hills; fruit trees and all cedars; wild animals and all livestock; small creatures and flying birds; kings of the earth and all peoples; princes and all judges of the earth; both young men and maidens; old men and children: let them praise Yahweh's name, for his name alone is exalted. His glory is above the earth and the heavens. (Psalm 148:7–13)

I see GOD in every glistening leaf shining in the sun. I hear Him in the songs of birds, some sweet, some loud, some long. I feel Him in a soft, lazy breeze, and I know He is here.

I observe the dragonfly as he hurries and flits about, searching for his food, never resting. I notice the intricacies of a spider's web in the morning dew and see evidence of our GOD. His handiwork amazes me. *My GOD, You are there in the 3D of my every day. Your ethereal Presence is everywhere. And it's You that I want to touch!*

I feel GOD in the warmth of sunlight, and I feel Him in the rain as it runs down my cheeks and slips into my mouth. I taste its sweet, refreshing goodness. I see joy in the loving exuberance of a puppy, so playful and innocent. I feel His sadness in the tears of a baby's cry. I see His power in the approaching storm clouds, threatening thunder and lightning bolts.

And after the storm, in the stillness of the night, I gaze up at the stars and am reminded of GOD's beauty and vastness. And the moon! I love to see that giant honey-coloured ball as it emerges above the horizon. *How big are You, oh Lord! All of this is a reminder of Your Presence and immense love for me.*

Can you see evidence of GOD? Can you feel Him? Reflect on what reminds you of your Heavenly Father. He'll be with you today. You just need to look.

Lord, may my eyes, ears and heart be more open and aware of how great You are, every day and everywhere. Help me to notice Your handiwork and be aware of Your presence and provision today. Amen

2

Sometimes

> For this, let everyone who is godly pray to you in a time when you may be found. Surely when the great waters overflow, they shall not reach to him. You are my hiding place. You will preserve me from trouble. You will surround me with songs of deliverance. Selah. (Psalm 32:6–7)

I had a precious dog, Bonnie, who sometimes wanted to receive lots of pats and attention. At other times, she would rather chase the noise of a neighbourhood gardener mowing his grass. Sometimes, I was too busy for a long pat, so I'd give her a comfort snack instead. When I was busy it was sometimes difficult to align the two – my time and her time to enjoy a cuddle.

It's like that in our relationship with GOD. As a busy day approaches, we read our Bibles quickly or else skip and hurriedly rush off. We justify that what we have to do is essential. 'GOD bless my day' and off we go.

But when we set aside time to meet with Him, and acknowledge Him, we can see His hand in our lives and enjoy His guidance more. Through spending time with our Father, we get to know His character. As we relate with Him, we become more aware of His guidance in our life. The result can only be blessings.

So, don't just fit time with GOD in with your bathroom and make-up duties. Start to set aside special time just for Him. He's there, and He promises to meet you. Your spirit will be enriched as you spend more time with your Heavenly Father!

Your Heavenly Father is constantly thinking about you. As you look around today, spend some time noticing His creation and provision for you.

Thank You, Father, that You are constantly with me, even when I'm not thinking about You. I'm sorry for the times that I have neglected You. Please help me to focus on You and spend time reading Your Word, so that I will learn more about Your character and goodness. Amen

3

Jewels

> Princes have persecuted me without a cause, but my heart stands in awe of your words. I rejoice at your word, as one who finds great plunder. I hate and abhor falsehood. I love your law. Seven times a day, I praise you, because of your righteous ordinances. Those who love your law have great peace. Nothing causes them to stumble. I have hoped for your salvation, Yahweh. I have done your commandments. My soul has observed your testimonies. I love them exceedingly. I have obeyed your precepts and your testimonies, for all my ways are before you.
> (Psalm 119:161–168)

I have some special 'gems' that have been shown to me by GOD himself throughout my life. They were often given to me in my darkest times when I was resting on a 'ledge" in a dark hole'. As the years passed, I gathered more of these beautiful gemstones. They were of varying sizes and shone different colours into my life as needed. As I held them, appreciated them and polished them, the stones would gleam, glow and reflect much-needed light! Light that was often not only illuminating but healing.

At times, I'd wear these 'gems' proudly and confidently, sharing them with others. The more that I obtained, the better they looked, and all together they became an extraordinary rainbow! People would appreciate them and be blessed by their beauty. Other times, they rested close to my hurting heart, warming and restoring me.

Now, no doubt you know I am speaking of GOD's precious promises and gems of wisdom in His blessed holy Word. As I read the Bible, I discovered, and still do, nourishing words of encouragement, instruction and words of promise. These stunning gems shine a light to me every day. These precious words sustain me and guide me through both the dark days and the bright days.

Some I commit to memory and some I write down to share with friends. As His precious children, we all would benefit from searching GOD's Word and storing it in our hearts so that we can reflect the heart of our Heavenly Father.

Do you have a favourite verse? Do you know it by heart? Why not write it down and take it with you today? Then tomorrow, do it again.

Lord GOD, create in me an inquisitiveness to seek You and discover new truths and promises in Your Word. Amen

4

Come Home

> Which of you men, if you had one hundred sheep, and lost one of them, wouldn't leave the ninety-nine in the wilderness, and go after the one that was lost, until he found it? When he has found it, he carries it on his shoulders, rejoicing. When he comes home, he calls together his friends and his neighbours, saying to them, 'Rejoice with me, for I have found my sheep which was lost!' I tell you that even so there will be more joy in heaven over one sinner who repents, than over ninety-nine righteous people who need no repentance. (Luke 15:4–7)

Something was going to happen. It was in the air! Darkness seemed to be coming upon us much earlier in the day than usual, so my daughter and I finalised our purchases quickly and commenced the 15-minute drive home. It was mid-afternoon, but it looked almost like night.

At last, I drove the car safely into the garage and we rushed inside to the protection of our home. *Whew!* Looking outside, it was so dark we could barely see our front street! The storm was close. The thunder was booming louder now.

And then it came! Loud, thunderous drops pelted the roof with bolts of lightning flashing across the gloomy sky! But we were both safe and dry inside. I felt concern for anyone who might be caught in this violent weather, and especially for those who don't know GOD's love. I pondered the safety of His love.

Quietly, my heart was saying, 'Come in from the rain! Don't you see it? Don't you feel it? It's getting heavier. Are you blinded by it? Are you used to it? Come into the cabin. There are dangers out there – falling debris could harm you and lightning could strike you! Come inside to the protection of GOD's love. We're all waiting for you, so come.'

Our loving Lord is waiting for you. All of Heaven rejoices over each one who returns, leaving the past behind. So, come to the Shepherd. His outstretched arms are longing and waiting for you to come home to the safety of His embrace. Come now and talk to the Shepherd.

 *Lord Jesus, I come. It's You that I need, and I choose You today, now and forever. Amen*

5

Thoughts

> For though we walk in the flesh, we don't wage war according to the flesh; for the weapons of our warfare are not of the flesh, but mighty before God to the throwing down of strongholds, throwing down imaginations and every high thing that is exalted against the knowledge of God and bringing every thought into captivity to the obedience of Christ, and being in readiness to avenge all disobedience when your obedience is made full. (2 Corinthians 10:3–6)

As a child, I loved reading comic books. I would read them for hours, enjoying their humour and pictures. In comic books spoken words are written in a balloon, with a pointer aiming at the speaker. And a character's thoughts are inside a bubble with smaller bubbles leading to the thinker. It's no wonder I tend to see thoughts as bubbles.

We women are constantly thinking, planning and organising our lives, family and workplace. We have kind thoughts, funny thoughts, good thoughts, mean thoughts and depressing thoughts. They come and they go. Just like bubbles floating in the breeze. Lots of them! What's in your thought bubble right now?

What is dominating your mind? Are you troubled with self-critical thoughts? Questioning your value or where you fit in? Low self-esteem is a problem for many of us.

It's possible to retrain your thoughts. It's called in the Bible 'the renewing of your mind' (Romans 12:2). As thoughts come to you, ask yourself, 'Are these healthy thoughts or negative thoughts?' The Holy Spirit speaks in quiet whispers and is never condemning. He is gentle and kind. GOD can help you to recognise what's from Him and what is not. Listen to your thoughts and take your guidance as you get to know Him better. He will speak, maybe quietly, so listen and do a self-check.

If a thought doesn't align with what you understand of GOD's character – for example, it is harmful to yourself or others – it is not from Him. You can pop that bubble right then and there and 'write' a new one. Choose now to bless as you are blessed. Practise good thinking deliberately. (Phil 4:8).

Take some time to observe and adjust what is in your thought bubbles throughout your day. Remember, you can realign your thinking with the Word of GOD and the prompting of His Holy Spirit.

Lord GOD, please guide my thoughts today so that I can understand and hear from You more clearly, and to recognise what is from You and what is not of You. Amen

6

Overall Design

> Aren't two sparrows sold for an assarion coin? Not one of them falls to the ground apart from your Father's will. But the very hairs of your head are all numbered. Therefore don't be afraid. You are of more value than many sparrows. (Matthew 10:29–31)

While trying to style my unruly hair into a nice, neat bob with my straightener, I noticed tiny niggling curls underneath not wanting to comply! These didn't show on the surface, but they did influence the behaviour of my style. They needed to be separated and ironed flat so that the result could be carefully coifed hair.

I began thinking about my life and saw a similarity. I tend to show others the neat, outward appearance, but just like my hair in rainy weather or humidity, the 'curls' always return. My hair is not so neat, and neither is my calm exterior. When the atmosphere changes, a little niggle of anger or envy pops out. I see the need to keep the Holy Spirit as my straightener to level out those inevitable strands of discord that arise from time to time when I least desire.

It's like this… My straightener is named 'Attitude', and as I give it into the Hands of the Holy Spirit, He smooths out the wrinkles and crinkles as much as I allow Him to. I need to see others in the light of Jesus' love for them. In GOD's word, we are told that we should 'Let your beauty be not just the outward adorning of braiding the hair, and of wearing jewels of gold, or of putting on fine clothing; but in the hidden person of the heart, in the incorruptible adornment of a gentle and quiet spirit, which is very precious in the sight of GOD. (1 Peter 3:3–4).

Let's think about attitude. We all have differing ones, some affected by hurts and worries. So let's permit the Holy Spirit to adjust ours to those that glorify our Father. This may take forgiveness and will require His help and grace. But it must be done to align with His loving plan for you.

Father, You know how many hairs are on my head. You know how many puffy, fluffy clouds float in the sky. You see it all and You watch over me too. You know all that I am feeling and thinking and doing. Oh, Lord, help me to hear the gentle corrections of the Holy Spirit and keep my eyes fixed on You, just as Yours are fixed on me. Amen

7

Vision

Not that I have already obtained, or am already made perfect; but I press on, that I may take hold of that for which also I was taken hold of by Christ Jesus. Brothers, I don't regard myself as yet having taken hold, but one thing I do: forgetting the things which are behind, and stretching forward to the things which are before, I press on toward the goal for the prize of the high calling of God in Christ Jesus. Let us therefore, as many as are perfect, think this way. If in anything you think otherwise, God will also reveal that to you. Nevertheless, to the extent that we have already attained, let's walk by the same rule. Let's be of the same mind. (Philippians 3:12–16)

I wear glasses. They help me to see with more clarity, so I can notice finer details. But if my glasses are foggy and in need of a clean, I find it difficult to focus and to clearly understand the picture right in front of me.

It's the same with my spiritual vision. Judgement, pride and unforgiveness can cloud my sight. The definition of what I am looking at becomes distorted and is not the clear truth or reality. My eyes deceive me. Through this vision, I could stumble, easily become hurt or, even worse, hurt others!

So, I must keep my spiritual glasses clear. The Holy Spirit Who is my filter and brings clarity to my vision and perception guides my steps. So then I have a safe daily walk in the right direction. I can keep my eyes on the prize. I am, and you are, an ordinary person with an extraordinary GOD living inside her.

Think about what you are going to be noticing today – what you will see and perceive. Will your vision be clear? Will you see the truth or your own limited perception? Let's look through the lens of GOD's love. Have a blessed day!

Thank You, Father, for Your Holy Spirit Who speaks and guides me as He arranges and rearranges my life. You, Lord, do it with such amazing precision. Amen

8

God-Shocked

But if while we sought to be justified in Christ, we ourselves also were found sinners, is Christ a servant of sin? Certainly not! For if I build up again those things which I destroyed, I prove myself a law-breaker. For I, through the law, died to the law, that I might live to God. I have been crucified with Christ, and it is no longer I who live, but Christ lives in me. That life which I now live in the flesh, I live by faith in the Son of God, who loved me, and gave himself up for me. I don't reject the grace of God. For if righteousness is through the law, then Christ died for nothing!" (Galatians 2:17–21)

I had a friend who encouraged me to read one of today's Bible verses. I had not been a Christian for long and she thought this would be good for me. So obediently I read Galatians 2:20: 'I have been crucified with Christ, and it is no longer I who live, but Christ lives in me. That life which I now live in the flesh, I live by faith in the Son of GOD, who loved me and gave Himself up for me.'

I came to know this verse very well and could quote all the words with confidence. But one day, while at work, I was data processing – a job that didn't require my full concentration – when voompah! A bomb went off inside me, or at least it felt like that. I hadn't moved, but my spirit inside certainly had. I received a clear message!

I instantly understood that I no longer had to *try* to live the Christian life; all I had to do was allow Jesus to live His life in and through me. That verse had suddenly impacted me so strongly that I knew the Holy Spirit had implanted the truth within me. A powerful but simple message delivered in a powerful way.

It's encouraging to know that that same power lives in all of us if we are believers. Allow Jesus, by the power of His Holy Spirit, to live in you today. Just trust. He's waiting for you now. It's as simple as this: When I die to my own desires, He lives in me, and when He lives in me, I live for Him.

Are you ready? He's there waiting. Permit that verse to come alive in you.

Thank You, Jesus, that You live inside me and that You have paved the way ahead. Help me to follow in the pathway as You lead. Amen

9

Baking

As they went on their way, he entered into a certain village, and a certain woman named Martha received him into her house. She had a sister called Mary, who also sat at Jesus' feet, and heard his word. But Martha was distracted with much serving, and she came up to him, and said, "Lord, don't you care that my sister left me to serve alone? Ask her therefore to help me." Jesus answered her, "Martha, Martha, you are anxious and troubled about many things, but one thing is needed. Mary has chosen the good part, which will not be taken away from her." (Luke 10:38–42)

Guests were coming and I was going to make a spectacular dessert – a decadent pavlova with all the trimmings. A soft, gooey meringue base would be topped with a layer of fresh, whipped cream and then luscious fruit. I had made this many times before and was sure it would be a delicious hit!

All was going great until I accidentally added bicarbonate of soda instead of baking powder to the meringue mixture. Realising it straight away, I carefully began to remove the delicate white powder from the top of the sticky, white mixture. It was like removing fine, crushed ice from the top of snow! Considering that I had it all out, or most of it, I then added the baking powder, mixed it in and gently tipped the mixture into a pan. I placed it onto an oven rack and waited for it to bake. Whew!

It rose beautifully like a delicious, floating cloud. I was feeling quite proud of my redeemed accomplishment. When it was done, I turned off the oven and removed the base to allow it to cool. However, as it did so, it changed from a 10-centimetre-high creation to a rather flat, large, white biscuit! *Oh, no!* I frisbeed it straight into the bin and rushed out to purchase one from a shop. This one I decorated as planned. It was not an original but still a very nice dessert.

What's the lesson here? The correct ingredients in our lives allow us to rise to our potential and make for a better result! Today, consider the ingredients that you are adding to your life. GOD's ingredients for a good life are found in reading His Word, praying to Him, spending time with Him and meeting with fellow believers. We then will reflect His love.

Father, as a chef follows the recipe for success, help me to follow Your pathway. Soften me to receive the good ingredients of Your loving guidance and directives, which will make me rise to become the person You plan for me to become, growing more into Your image. Amen

Pavlova

Ingredients:
- 2 egg whites
- 1 ½ cups caster sugar
- 2 teaspoons vinegar
- 2 teaspoons vanilla
- 3 teaspoons baking powder (NOT baking soda)
- 4 tablespoons of boiling water

Method:
1. Add sugar to egg white.
2. Add vinegar to mixture and beat for two minutes.
3. Add vanilla to mixture and beat for two minutes.
4. Add boiling water and beat for ten minutes.
5. When mixture is stiff, fold in baking powder (I usually add this before the ten minutes is up.)
6. Place on a pie dish or loose-based baking pan, lined with baking paper.
7. Bake in a slow oven (140 C or 275 F) for about one hour or until it appears done, crusty on the outside and soft inside. It should be hard when you tap it. It will drop just a little in size as it cools.
8. Allow to cool completely and top with whipped cream and your choice of fresh fruit. Serve immediately.

Servings: 6–8

Note: This recipe is best prepared with a free-standing mixer, or else your device will get hot. This recipe is suitable to halve, using only one egg white for a smaller result, but equally as delicious! It can be prepared a day earlier but leave the adding of the toppings until just before serving. Have fun! It's a never-fail dessert!

10

Washing Up

> Have mercy on me, God, according to your loving kindness. According to the multitude of your tender mercies, blot out my transgressions. Wash me thoroughly from my iniquity. Cleanse me from my sin. For I know my transgressions. (Psalm 51:1–3)

One day, while washing up the dishes, I accidentally added too much detergent to the water. There were bubbles everywhere! But, since I had begun, I kept going, disregarding the intense effervescent problem. I figured the dishes would get clean, and even though it was difficult, it was kind of fun!

It was a slippery effort on my part, and then I noticed that some shiny plates had spots on them despite all the bubbles! They needed re-washing, which I then had to do. Lots of thoughts came to me as I scrubbed and rubbed. It's amazing what wanders through your mind when doing ordinary jobs.

I began considering how some of us try to conceal our secret spots by bubbly personalities or effervescent chatter. And some of us attempt to hide these spots by our own efforts. We use makeup to conceal hidden flaws, or choose the latest hairstyle or colours, wearing expensive clothing to satisfy a need. Some of us drive fancy cars, live in big homes and have amazing holidays. None of this is wrong, but if we're looking for happiness in doing these, it will elude us.

For some of us, these things all seem to assist in making us feel successful, comparing our lives to those of others. But let's not be tricked, for only true fulfilment will arrive as we submit and permit ourselves to go through GOD's cleaner to remove all spots and rubbish away. He uses the Blood of Christ to cleanse and sanctify. As we go to Him for forgiveness, true and lasting cleansing washes over us and we are made like new!

True peace and joy come from the Author of Life. So let's face our concerns, be honest and look to Him. This is your chance today to be effervescent with His joy that will stay.

Help me to remember, Father, that I don't need to self-remedy with things and desires that I don't need. Acquisitions don't bring permanent happiness. Only my Maker can do that, so I will seek You first in all things. Amen

11

Ice Cream

> The grace of the Lord Jesus Christ, God's love, and the fellowship of the Holy Spirit be with you all. Amen. (2 Corinthians 13:14)

As the Holy Spirit comes into our lives, we are blessed with a new sense of peace and joy. We feel complete and satisfied. It's a wonderful feeling and we must be careful not to lose it. Only offenses can cause this feeling to leave, so we must be careful to avoid hurting someone or being easily offended and unforgiving. Otherwise the voice of the Holy Spirit can't be heard for the din of discordance. It's something like this story...

You are given an ice cream in a cone labelled 'Salvation'. You choose your favourite flavours to fill the cone to overflowing. Let's do three scoops! On the top, place some sweets, then drizzle melted chocolate and lastly top it off with a shiny red cherry. Doesn't that look delicious, like the most appealing dessert ever? Can you imagine it?

Now, you are told that you must carry it over to your family picnic, but not to spill a single drop of ice cream or sweets. You walk slowly, being careful to not stumble or trip over any unseen danger.

In a similar way, this is how we are to host or carry the Holy Spirit in our lives. Remember, He is part of the GODhead. All three are one; Father, Son and Holy Spirit are beautifully woven together like your three favourite ice creams – and they are inseparable. If you have invited Jesus in, the Holy Spirit lives inside you. So carry Him carefully, watching out for temptations and warnings, and He will remain, fellowshipping with you.

Just as an ice cream will lose its flavour and melt, temptations of any kind like petty jealousy or offenses, which hurt your pride, will cause your fellowship to slip away

These words are for you today. Savour them. It's your choice whether you will share your joy. Like that delectable and desirable ice cream, everyone needs this! How will you carry your blessings today?

 *Lord GOD, may Your grace, mercy and peace be seen in me as I carry Your goodness around in my human frame today. Amen*

12

Daffodils

> As for man, his days are like grass. As a flower of the field, so he flourishes.
> For the wind passes over it, and it is gone. Its place remembers it no more.
> But Yahweh's loving kindness is from everlasting to everlasting with those who fear him, his righteousness to children's children, to those who keep his covenant, to those who remember to obey his precepts. (Psalm 103:15–18)

I try to be careful while I shop, so I've developed a theory: I don't need everything that I like. This helps me to assess whether I'm being materialistic, desiring things that appeal to my eyes and then regretting the overspending. It's easy to tell myself that I've worked hard and deserve it, but is that a good enough reason to make that purchase? Not always. So, I try to choose wisely and invite the Lord to shop with me. This makes me a smarter buyer, and sometimes He guides me to bargains. That's a plus!

On the way home from work one day, I quickly dashed into my local supermarket to grab a few supplies as guests were coming over that night. As I was leaving, I noticed some beautiful daffodils for sale. Despite thinking how gorgeous they were and that they reminded me of my mother, I still decided to resist the temptation to buy and hurriedly walked out. But then I heard the soft voice of the Holy Spirit saying to get them as they may bless someone at the meeting tonight. So I raced back and bought them, and I dutifully displayed them in a vase on a blue tablecloth. They looked stunning, but nobody seemingly noticed them.

The next morning, as I was reading my Bible and having a quiet time with my Lord, I remembered that experience and asked Him what it was all about. Then I received the insight that He had told me to buy the daffodils as a gift for me! It's strange but GOD wanted *me* to have those daffodils. He wanted to bless me.

Our Father desires to bless His children in many ways. This was my blessing that day and I felt so special to Him! How good is GOD! How kind!

Look around and listen. You just never know what He might be saying to you, and what He wants to bless you with.

Lord Jesus, You amaze me! Thank You for your goodness and your loving kindness to me. Let me be aware of your gifts this day. Amen

13

Succulent Delight

"I am the true vine, and my Father is the farmer. Every branch in me that doesn't bear fruit, he takes away. Every branch that bears fruit, he prunes, that it may bear more fruit. You are already pruned clean because of the word which I have spoken to you. Remain in me, and I in you. As the branch can't bear fruit by itself unless it remains in the vine, so neither can you, unless you remain in me. I am the vine. You are the branches. He who remains in me and I in him bears much fruit, for apart from me you can do nothing. If a man doesn't remain in me, he is thrown out as a branch and is withered; and they gather them, throw them into the fire, and they are burned. If you remain in me, and my words remain in you, you will ask whatever you desire, and it will be done for you. In this my Father is glorified, that you bear much fruit; and so you will be my disciples." (John 15: 1–8)

I was relaxing after a morning cup of coffee one day, admiring some cute succulents that I had potted in cups and saucers, when I thought that I should tidy them up. As I lifted the leaves of one, I discovered dead growth underneath. After removing the dead leaves, I noticed that it stood taller, not leaning or bending over. I then saw the need to prune other plants.

Doing this prune made the plants appear prettier and stronger, without the weight of old, dry leaves. I pondered how removing old decaying foliage and subsequent pruning, even on new growth, is just what is needed for plants to grow in the right direction, upwards and onwards.

What about us? Do we need pruning sometimes? Can you see a parallel? Our Heavenly Father is the True Gardener. He always knows what He is doing. His good purpose is always for *our* good purpose. And sometimes a little pain brings the best result as He removes some unbeneficial growths in our lives, which could hinder our upward and onward journey. It may not be pleasant, but it is always worthwhile.

Is there something about yourself, or your life, that needs cleaning and clearing? Perhaps a bad habit or attitude? Perhaps something you need to leave in the past where it belongs? Consider asking the Holy Spirit today to make you aware of what you need to let go of. Allow GOD to do His good Work in you.

Father, make me more aware of what things need to be pruned in me and in my life. Just as the plant gets its life and strength from the sap, help me to draw my life and strength through the Blood of Jesus for cleansing and growing. Amen

14

Prickles

He answered them, "He who sows the good seed is the Son of Man, the field is the world, the good seeds are the children of the Kingdom, and the darnel weeds are the children of the evil one. The enemy who sowed them is the devil. The harvest is the end of the age, and the reapers are angels. As therefore the darnel weeds are gathered up and burned with fire; so will it be at the end of this age. The Son of Man will send out his angels, and they will gather out of his Kingdom all things that cause stumbling and those who do iniquity, and will cast them into the furnace of fire. There will be weeping and gnashing of teeth. Then the righteous will shine like the sun in the Kingdom of their Father. He who has ears to hear, let him hear. (Matthew 13: 37–43)

Early one day, while wandering around in my garden, I noticed some Cobbler's Pegs hiding amongst some of my plants. These are nasty weeds, so I decided to pull them out. As I investigated further, I saw more, so out they came too! *In the bin you go!* My satisfaction at dumping them in the bin was short-lived as I felt something prickling my feet and legs. To my great dislike, I found there were many more

Cobbler's Pegs stuck to my slippers and dressing gown! I duly pulled these off. Investigating still further, I discovered that they were even more sneakily stuck to my clothing everywhere!

It took ages to remove them – a painstaking, tedious process. The insidious, tiny, sticky barbs, which entwined like crochet hooks, were black. And except for some white flowers, so was my dressing gown. Horrors!

Just like a nasty attitude or bad behaviour, I thought. Non-loving thoughts and behaviours similarly creep up and stick – invisible but prickly, uncomfortable and so difficult to remove. How do we get rid of a bad attitude, habit or behaviour?

We need GOD for that job. He specialises with removal of sticky problems. We can come to Him, asking for forgiveness and love, and He will fully cleanse us. This comes as we trust Jesus to forgive our past and to cleanse and change us, making us like brand new!

Are you needing a clean, fresh start today? It's just a prayer away.

Father, thank You for the freedom and forgiveness I can experience through the blood of Jesus. Amen

15

Surprise Attack!

Put on therefore, as God's chosen ones, holy and beloved, a heart of compassion, kindness, lowliness, humility, and perseverance; bearing with one another, and forgiving each other, if any man has a complaint against any; even as Christ forgave you, so you also do.

Above all these things, walk in love, which is the bond of perfection. And let the peace of God rule in your hearts, to which also you were called in one body, and be thankful. Let the word of Christ dwell in you richly; in all wisdom teaching and admonishing one another with psalms, hymns, and spiritual songs, singing with grace in your heart to the Lord.

Whatever you do, in word or in deed, do all in the name of the Lord Jesus, giving thanks to God the Father, through him. (Colossians 3:12–17)

I had chosen to make corn and bacon soup for our weekend evening meal. Yummy! But with no can of corn in the pantry, I put my dog Bonnie on her lead and off we went for a nice, quick walk to the local store. As we approached the store, I noticed a man putting a lead on a large black dog near the entrance. I felt it safe to secure Bonnie to the handle of a vacant shop next door, some distance away from the black dog. I ducked inside to make my purchase. While paying for that can, I heard a dog fight outside! I quickly raced out, just in time to observe with horror the black dog attacking Bonnie, with the man holding the lead! Poor Bonnie wasn't even retaliating.

I yelled and the dog fight broke up, the man then withdrawing his dog. Upon inspecting Bonnie, I saw blood on her ear and face. I told the man that he would have to pay the vet bill, which he agreed to do. But in the trauma of the moment, he hurriedly sneaked away into an awaiting car and took off. I was furious!

After a desperate phone call, my husband drove down and we rushed to the animal hospital, which resulted in an operation and an overnight stay for one traumatised dog. The next day, and one thousand dollars later, we brought our whimpering, precious pet back home. Everyone was glad that it was over but upset and angry. I felt crushed.

I reported the incident to my local council but had no name or address to give to them. So the complaint couldn't be registered. I felt destroyed in my spirit. I just wanted to crawl away and die, but GOD said, 'Let it go. You must forgive'. At first, I thought he meant this one-off offence. Oh no… GOD wanted me to forgive *all* the offences that had occurred against me throughout my whole life. This one was only the beginning.

GOD began to take me on a journey and revealed to me the other unforgiven offences. One by one, He brought them to remembrance, and I forgave them. It was only with His help that I even began the process. Ultimately, it would free me.

Sometime later, when I was walking along with my dog, I crossed paths with that same man again with his dog. I discovered that I had absolutely no animosity towards him. I knew then that GOD had healed my unforgiving spirit. What a change was brought about by a terrible incident.

Consider the offences that you may hold onto. Would forgiveness release you too? You are not alone in this, and forgiveness is necessary for you to move along in your faith walk with Him. He'll walk with you through all of this. Trust Him.

Thank You, Lord. You have forgiven me, and now I see value in other people. I now know it is obedient, with Your help, to forgive them also because all people are precious to You. Amen

16

Impossible Forgiveness

Pray like this:

"'Our Father in heaven, may your name be kept holy.
Let your Kingdom come.
 Let your will be done on earth as it is in heaven.
Give us today our daily bread.
Forgive us our debts,
 as we also forgive our debtors.
Bring us not into temptation,
 but deliver us from the evil one.

For yours is the Kingdom, the power, and the glory forever. Amen.'[a]
"For if you forgive men their trespasses, your heavenly Father will also forgive you. But if you don't forgive men their trespasses, neither will your Father forgive your trespasses. (Matthew 6:9–15)

What had happened in our lives was devastating, and I knew I had to forgive my ex-husband, the father of my children. It was required of me by GOD for my walk with Him to continue in harmony. And it was obedience to Him. But what this man had done was terrible! Not just injuring me, causing intense emotional hurt, but also my children, His children! GOD knew. GOD understood the extreme pain and His heart ached for His children too. Our Father was watching and feeling our pain as we bore the consequences of this man's evil actions.

How could I forgive him?

A promise came. I read in the Book of Daniel, chapter three, that Shadrack, Meshack and Abed Nego came through the fiery furnace without even the smell of smoke on them. 'Thanks, Lord,' I said, feeling desperate. 'I'll trust You for that one!' I claimed it. But I was still struggling to forgive this horrible transgression against all of us! Nothing like this had ever happened to me before, and the pain felt like the worst thing in history, my history anyway.

I then read in the Lord's Prayer that it's necessary to forgive others first if we request forgiveness for ourselves from GOD, our Father. (Matt 6:12–15) Jesus forgave every single sinner as He died on the cross, not just for my sins but for everyone's – without exception. That is, if they ask for it. In my desperate need, at this point, GOD showed His Hand in a vision to me. I knew that if I put my hand into His, forgiveness would immediately be possible. Very humbly, I did this, and as I trusted Him to help, He did!

Forgiveness set me free from my pain. It was like breathing real air again. I was freed and felt brand new. My family and I had a tough road to travel, but we were on it with GOD leading the way. Forgiveness is for everyone, and GOD Himself can help you with the toughies!

Do you have any unresolved forgiveness? Ask GOD – He's there to help you.

 *Lord GOD, You know how hard it has been to let go of the hurts that have crippled me inside. Please take them now, and by Your Grace, I forgive those offenders. Restore to me the joy of Your salvation. Amen*

17

Heights

> In nothing be anxious, but in everything, by prayer and petition with thanksgiving, let your requests be made known to God. And the peace of God, which surpasses all understanding, will guard your hearts and your thoughts in Christ Jesus. (Philippians 4:6–7)

I don't like heights. My fear began as a little girl when my dad warned me of the dangers and consequences of being too close to a cliff edge. On a family holiday, my husband, daughter and I decided to go to the top of Mt Wellington. Because of my sensitivity to heights, we decided that I should drive as it would give me a sense of control. Famous last words!

Off I began the upward incline. As we proceeded, the road became narrower, and the curves increased. At one stage, I noticed the apex far into the distance and realised that I had a long way to go. My palms started to sweat, and my hands gripped the steering wheel more tightly as I leaned closer to it. My heart was beating faster, and I was becoming more agitated. I drove the car very slowly, close to the rocky cliff face of the mountain, even though it was the wrong side of the road. I was terrified of falling over the edge!

Hugging close to the mountain in this fashion, I was still feeling frantic. My passengers were also – because of my driving. They wanted me to pull over. Terrified though I was, I kept driving. Too scared to stop the car, I just wanted to reach the summit, which eventually we did.

Feeling so tense after that ordeal, yet relieved, I refused to even look at the incredible view from the mountain top because I knew I had to drive down again. My husband and daughter went to have a look and to take photos. They perhaps quietly celebrated that they had made it up alive.

Not surprisingly, I was not permitted to drive down and was gently led into the back seat. Earphones were placed on my head and my favourite Christian song was played for me to listen to. On the safe descent, I listened to that song four times while I cried and prayed all the way down.

This had been a genuine panic attack. My first. It was real and unbelievably terrifying, based on a realistic fear, which my mind had blown out of proportion. I learned from that experience that it's not good to be a control freak.

Can you relate to this experience? My advice is to give all your unknown fears to a known GOD. He will never let you down. Give GOD the controls and He will guide you safely on your journey. Remember, most of the things that we fear never happen anyway.

I praise you, my Father, that your comforting love and protection is always there for me to abide in. Help me to reach out to you in faith when I feel overwhelmed by fears and anxieties, knowing you are close by. Amen

18

Deliverance

> Don't remember the former things, and don't consider the things of old. Behold, I will do a new thing. It springs out now. Don't you know it? I will even make a way in the wilderness, and rivers in the desert. (Isaiah 43:18–19)

Have you had a delivery of something unexpected? Was it a nice delivery or not to your liking? Deliverance can take on many forms. You may not even recognise it when it swoops down to get you. A sudden change of circumstances catches you off guard quite unexpectedly, changing your life forever! You may experience a removal from a situation that you had not even recognised as dangerous or critical. The deliverance can be a rescue.

It's in the deliverance that renewal comes. It happens at the perfect time. GOD's time! This rescuing may not be convenient for us, but He has our attention now. It's GOD's timing, and in His time we may understand.

Even if you never comprehend the reasoning behind such an event, understand that it all will eventually assist you to grow just a little bit more into the image of Jesus, bit by bit. His guiding, protecting Hand will carry, sustain and protect you. His way is perfect. As He leads, just follow Him. The pathway is safe, for He has walked it before you.

Learning, growth and change will occur in the process of following. So, take another step on the next paver along the way. It may seem unsafe, but it's there for you and it is safe. Jesus understands. He has walked this pathway before you, and He holds your hand.

The way is ahead for you. Will you take another step?

Thank You, Father, that You hold me in Your Hand. I can move around in Your hand, yet I am safe. Your hand is soft and is a comfort to me. As I look up in worship, I feel Your loving gaze upon me. As You envelop me and keep me in Your gentle grip, I feel protected and loved. Amen

19

Hidden Blessings

> For we were saved in hope, but hope that is seen is not hope. For who hopes for that which he sees? But if we hope for that which we don't see, we wait for it with patience. In the same way, the Spirit also helps our weaknesses, for we don't know how to pray as we ought. But the Spirit himself makes intercession for us with groanings which can't be uttered. He who searches the hearts knows what is on the Spirit's mind, because he makes intercession for the saints according to God. (Romans 8:24–27)

Life doesn't always go smoothly for all of us. Can you remember a time in your life when a cataclysmic event occurred? Are you going through one now? At some point in our lives, 'bad things' will occur. We do not expect them. They just arrive – abrupt and disturbing interludes stopping us in our tracks! It can feel like a tree suddenly falling across a perfectly plain pathway. At other times, unchosen events can creep slowly into our awareness, and we are unprepared for the shock as we discover them.

These things can be the loss of someone precious, a relationship breakdown, a child's health scare, or financial or work issues. They all come in different packaging. Some people see GOD as responsible for such unwanted events and blame Him, in anger. Still others reach out to Him desperately. They ask, 'Why did this happen?' and 'What have I done to deserve this?'

This I know: It's not our business to know why it happened. Simply trust GOD. He permitted this apparent calamity, and He will bring about His purpose in and through it. He will get the glory as His will unfolds in our lives. This was my experience after the shocking events in my life I shared in my story. I discovered His goodness and kindness as I yielded to Him, trusting Him for the outcome. His enduring faithfulness and love guided me into my future, and He will do the same for you. Without all that I have been through, I wouldn't be talking to you right now.

It's in the valley, and in the pain, that you'll find the best fertilizer and the most fertile soil. That's where you grow best as you lean on Him for nourishment and strength. In due time, while you would never look back and ask for such an event to occur, you will see it has been an enriching experience. You have gotten to know your Heavenly Father much more intimately. The 'interlude' has been entirely worthwhile.

If you are in that place, keep trusting, keep believing and rest in Him. As you do, you will get through this because you are never alone. GOD is with you. Remember, all things work for the good of those that love the Lord.

Thank You, Father. You are my guiding Hand. You are right here and have been all along! You are worthy of my trust! Amen

20

Detour

> Enter in by the narrow gate; for the gate is wide and the way is broad that leads to destruction, and there are many who enter in by it. How narrow is the gate and the way is restricted that leads to life! There are few who find it. (Matthew 7:13–14)

Have you ever been travelling in your car when suddenly traffic comes to a grinding halt? Perhaps it's road works or an accident. But there you are, caught in it and moving so slow, if at all. How frustrating and inconvenient! But you resign to the fact that you are now going to be late.

Similarly, travelling on the road of life, sometimes you are slowed down considerably from going your own way. Then you see a sign: 'GOD'S DETOUR'. So since you really need to get to your destination, you begin to travel on a different road.

GOD intervened in my life in a big way, rescuing my kids and me from a detrimental situation. Suddenly, life took a different direction. In that experience, I learned to know Him better and to understand His guidance. Not knowing where we were headed was tricky but rewarding as I could see that our future was in safe, strong Hands.

GOD had taken us on a detour to a new pathway, sometimes seemingly a downward one for a time being. But I trusted Him, and it proved good. I learned a lot about Him at that time.

As we re-emerged onto that highway of life, there was a calmness and confidence somewhere inside. I could clearly see that the Son had been shining on us the whole time!

Can you recall an unintentional delay or change in your life that has worked out for the better? Recognise His presence and His leading and thank Him for being there.

Lord, I have learned that when things go my way, and sometimes don't go my way, YOU are with me all the way. You are working out Your plans to perfect me into the Christ follower that You want me to become. Your way, YAHWEH, is perfect. It's all about You, Jesus!

Just Trust

Hard times will come, and you will despair,
But reach to the Lord; He's always there.
He'll guide and lead you as you trust in His Word.
Just follow each step – none is absurd.

Life may seem tricky and each pill hard to swallow;
But don't choke, just believe, as you trustingly follow.
You will emerge from this place you didn't understand
With new strength, new resolve as GOD has your hand.
There's a purpose for this and not knowing the reason,
You've discovered His power, now you'll thrive in each season.

So if adversity comes and surely it will,
Reach up to Jesus whose sacrifice on the hill
Will lead you to victory as you submit to Him,
Your debt paid on a tree by His nail-pierced limbs.

Sherylle Grace Wells

21

Timely Rescue

> It will happen that before they call, I will answer; and while they are yet speaking, I will hear. (Isaiah 65:24)

It was Boxing Day 1983, and my extended family had met for a belated Christmas celebration. Being a beautiful sunny day at the beach, after exchanging gifts many of us hit the water. Being 35 weeks pregnant, I chose to stay with my daughter, mum, sister and niece on the sandy shore of the Maroochy River. There we sat and chatted, giggled and enjoyed splashes of the cool water. As we headed back, we noticed a group of people gathering. Curious, we had a look. Through the crowd, we could see a man lying in the recovery position on his side in a small boat. It was Dad!

A nurse, hearing our cries, appeared and explained to us that a strong, young man from Thursday Island had been watching my dad bobbing around in the river. When Dad didn't resurface, he went into the river to rescue him. His body was a dead weight and too heavy. There just 'happened' to be a young boy nearby who was trying out his new Christmas gift, a surf ski. Dad was placed on top and floated into shore, not far from where we had been sitting.

There 'happened' to be two trained nurses on the beach that day who administered CPR and got breath into my dad. There also 'happened' to be a rowboat nearby for him to be placed inside so that the rescue could continue towards the nearest hospital. After four days in ICU, my dad made a full recovery except for the loss of his bottom dentures. He joked that a fish was probably swimming in the river with a big smile.

My prayers changed from that day. I used to always pray for Dad's salvation. Now that I knew he had experienced physical salvation, I prayed more specifically for his *spiritual* salvation. I prayed this until the day he died, 12 years later. I then learned that Dad had told Mum that when he had drowned all those years before, he'd gone through a dark tunnel. He later admitted to our local pastor that he'd also acknowledged Jesus in that tunnel. His favourite song from then on became *Shine Jesus Shine*. I guess if you met Jesus in His Heavenly bright light, it would be a perfect choice.

Learning of Dad's experience with Jesus in that tunnel taught me that we only need to take a tiny step towards Jesus for Him to reach for us and grab us, bringing us into His Heavenly Kingdom. I also understood that GOD had truly listened and attended to my continual prayer. (Psalms 66:19) I'm now expecting to see my dad in Heaven with my mum when I get to that Glorious Land.

Make sure you're prepared. Pray for your loved ones who aren't yet saved. Life can change dramatically in the twinkling of an eye.

Father, I thank You for Your loving providence that is always with me. For You go before me and prepare that unknown path ahead. You answer prayers before I know I need to pray them, and I know my way is safe. Amen

22

Midnight Awakening

> Don't you know that your bodies are members of Christ? Shall I then take the members of Christ and make them members of a prostitute? May it never be! Or don't you know that he who is joined to a prostitute is one body? For, "The two", he says, "will become one flesh." But he who is joined to the Lord is one spirit. Flee sexual immorality! "Every sin that a man does is outside the body," but he who commits sexual immorality sins against his own body. Or don't you know that your body is a temple of the Holy Spirit who is in you, whom you have from God? You are not your own, for you were bought with a price. Therefore glorify God in your body and in your spirit, which are God's. (1 Corinthians 6:15–20)

As a young single again mum after divorce, I was feeling lonely and missing companionship and conversation within marriage. This was a struggle in my now sole parent role, and I felt I needed an adult to talk with. One day, I noticed an ad in the local newspaper for a man wanting to meet a single lady. On impulse, I answered that ad. Soon afterwards we met one night for coffee at a coffee shop.

It seemed a good evening of conversation. After about one and a half hours, we exchanged phone numbers – I must have met with his approval as he wanted to arrange a dinner date – and we parted company. I then went home to my mother's house where I had left my two young children. Mum had very kindly looked after them and bedded them before I returned to sleep at her place. All seemed well and I went to bed, with thoughts of school and work the next day.

In the early hours of the next morning, I was awakened to a noise from my young son. Not wanting to disturb the household, I hurriedly went to him. While I was still walking down the hallway, I heard a strong, impressionable voice within me. The voice spoke very clearly about 'aligning light with darkness' and about 'prostituting the Body of Christ with evil'.

This hit me powerfully. I knew what I had to do. There and then, at that early hour, I resolved to end this friendship before it began – to nip it in the bud. I considered and understood the risks and possible danger involved, firstly, to my two children and to my walk with the Lord.

The next day, I rang the man to let him know that I was a Christian and could not go out with him as we were not equally yoked. This puzzled him and he replied that he was okay with my Christianity and could accommodate it. He might even attend church! I apologised to him, but it was difficult to get out of a meeting that had been so easy to get into.

I finally understood GOD's point to me: If you can't relate from deep within you, from your soul to another's, you've got nothing. I realised that I needed someone who could share GOD's heart with me and together we could understand each other. Then the relationship could grow.

In His time, I did meet a lovely Christian man whom I could share my soul with, and later in that marriage we had a daughter.

This is my lesson and warning to you. Be careful not to make the big mistake that I almost did. But, if you are in that place, know that you've not been abandoned by GOD. Talk to Him. He'll forgive, restore and guide you. There is hope as GOD meets us where we are at – always. Whether we're already in a relationship or not, He has not forgotten you and loves you both. Remember, GOD can work all things for the good of all who love him (Rom. 8:28).

Lord, I trust You to bring the right friendships and relationships that I need into my life. Be ever present with me and help me to share Your love with people I love so that Your influence brings comfort and change to their lives too. Amen

23

Sequence Of Events

> Be subject therefore to God. Resist the devil, and he will flee from you. Draw near to God, and he will draw near to you. Cleanse your hands, you sinners. Purify your hearts, you double-minded. Lament, mourn, and weep. Let your laughter be turned to mourning, and your joy to gloom. Humble yourselves in the sight of the Lord, and he will exalt you. (James 4: 7–10)

One morning, I opened my servery window, something I do every day, when I noticed something different. Movement! *What's that?* I looked again and saw a gecko on my kitchen bench – quite a large gecko. I decided that it needed to be outside! It was right next to the open window, so I hurried along its departure to the outside world where it belonged, shooing it with a handy bottle. Not the best choice, but it was close by.

The gecko was one centimetre or so from its escape, but it froze, terrified, and would not take the leap up and over the windowsill. My husband Robin heard the kitchen chaos and arrived in time to hand me a catalogue. That did the trick! Gary Gecko – I now had given it a name, feeling sorry for the poor thing – at last made the leap and was now outside, sitting on the brick window frame.

I closed the window again, the sound of which caused him to leap from the sill to, hopefully, safety. Goodbye, you're gone! However, as I went to go outside through my doorway, I again saw Gary floating on top of the water in the dog's water bucket. He was not swimming!

Urgently, I called for Robin's assistance again. He quickly scooped him up and placed him on the pergola floor. Sadly, along came my dog, curious about the commotion and stepped on the poor thing's tail! The little guy was still moving, so Robin relocated him to a safe spot in the garden. I haven't seen him since and hope that he restored from his adventurous escapade and moved to a safer household.

Just as Samson found himself in danger in the presence of Delilah, we need to be careful where we find ourselves. Make clear, safe choices about where we go, and remain listening to GOD. Unseen dangers are all around us, although often very subtle. Think about where you're going today. It's a big world out there. Choose wisely who your friends are and what you will see. It's so easy to be found in the wrong place at the wrong time and then end up in danger just like Gary the little gecko.

Be intentional with your choices and always honour GOD, and He will honour you.

Lord, thank You for Your protection and guidance. Help me to go where You want me to go today and to be aware that the devil is out there like a roaring lion trying to ensnare me or a sneaky snake trying to trick me.

Amen

24

Christian Ducks

Why do you say, Jacob, and speak, Israel, "My way is hidden from Yahweh, and the justice due me is disregarded by my God?"

Haven't you known? Haven't you heard? The everlasting God, Yahweh, the Creator of the ends of the earth, doesn't faint.

He isn't weary. His understanding is unsearchable. He gives power to the weak. He increases the strength of him who has no might.

Even the youths faint and get weary, and the young men utterly fall;
but those who wait for Yahweh will renew their strength.

They will mount up with wings like eagles. They will run, and not be weary. They will walk, and not faint. (Isaiah 40:27–31)

While sitting at a park one day, I watched giggling children amusing themselves by throwing bits of bread to some hungry ducks. As more bread landed on the surface of the pond, more of these hungry creatures would swim nearer to get their share. It caused quite a commotion amongst the birdlife population as other ducks kept drawing closer. The children were all delighted. But then the bread was gone, so life was restored to normal again.

I had found the activity playing out in front of me very entertaining. Then I began to consider that some of us Christians are like ducks. Ducks are content to simply peck away at food as they graze around their surroundings. They swim and they paddle, enjoying the pond and the company of other ducks.

As Christians, we are often content to mill around together, chatting after church, and then simply get back to our daily lives. But we are not meant to simply sit around. We are meant to fly! It's when ducks are roused or frightened that they zoom up to incredible heights at tremendous speed, and their true beauty is revealed. The same for us.

As precious saved ones, we need to continue to grow and soar with Jesus, not only when a tragic situation arises but all the time. Don't wait for a crisis; be prepared for your future. Reach out to others in their crisis. It's then that you will achieve what you have been created to do. Don't wait until you've been stirred to action by pressure. Test those wings! Fly now!

Are you ready? GOD wants to lift your wings today and fly with you.

Lord GOD, make me to rise as on wings of eagles, to fly high, knowing that You are the enabling GOD Who makes me to soar. Amen

25

The Lazy Sheepdog

> Jesus therefore said to them again, "Most certainly, I tell you, I am the sheep's door. All who came before me are thieves and robbers, but the sheep didn't listen to them. I am the door. If anyone enters in by me, he will be saved, and will go in and go out, and will find pasture. The thief only comes to steal, kill, and destroy. I came that they may have life, and may have it abundantly. I am the good shepherd. The good shepherd lays down his life for the sheep. (John 10:7–11)

One day a shepherd calls out to his sheepdog, 'Go to those sheep!' to stop them going over a cliff. The sheepdog won't listen, and the sheep keep on eating the grass, unaware of the danger nearby. The shepherd again commands, 'Go over there!' But the dog simply rolls over. *Did I hear something?*

Some of the sheep nibble slightly closer to the edge. After all, the grass closer to the cliff edge is greener and tastier. 'GO!' calls the shepherd.

The dog? *What! Did you say something?* as he is roused from his nap. The group wanders even closer and suddenly a lamb loses its footing. Finally alarmed, the dog runs toward the lamb, but it is too late!

Just then, another older sheepdog rushes to the edge and, barking wildly, shoos the remaining sheep back to the safety of the paddock and into the fold. But what happens to the lamb? Sadly, he is gone. The first sheepdog hasn't been alert.

The job of sheepdogs is to guard and protect the sheep on behalf of its shepherd. They normally love to serve their master for the reward of a pat, and at the end of the day, a hearty feast and bed for the night. Jesus is often referred to as the Shepherd and so we often think of us ourselves as his flock. But have you ever considered we have a role to play in guarding his flock too? He did instruct Peter to feed his sheep. As so we must too.

Are you listening to your Shepherd today and obeying His instructions? Are you watching out for the flock and the lost lambs? Where are the lost lambs? Are they in your neighbourhood, down the street, across the world? The Bible says we all, like sheep, have gone astray. Each of us has turned his own way. It's our duty to serve our Shepherd and round them up, leading them into the Fold.

Be careful to watch out for the sheep and lambs today.

Lord, help me to notice people that You place on my path today. Help me to see their needs and not to 'sleep on the job' or be too busy to reach out. You have put Your message of life and love inside me. Teach me how to share! Amen

26

Sculptures

Yahweh said to Moses, "I will do this thing also that you have spoken; for you have found favour in my sight, and I know you by name."

Moses said, "Please show me your glory."

He said, "I will make all my goodness pass before you, and will proclaim Yahweh's name before you. I will be gracious to whom I will be gracious, and will show mercy on whom I will show mercy." He said, "You cannot see my face, for man may not see me and live." Yahweh also said, "Behold, there is a place by me, and you shall stand on the rock. It will happen, while my glory passes by, that I will put you in a cleft of the rock, and will cover you with my hand until I have passed by; then I will take away my hand, and you will see my back; but my face shall not be seen." (Exodus 33:17–23)

Have you seen ancient churches and cathedrals with stain glassed windows and magnificent columns and statues? The workmanship is impressive and exquisite. Such detail has gone into the creation of these beautiful works including statues of Jesus and his mother Mary.

And what about paintings. Just think of Leonardo da Vinci's *The Last Supper* and Michelangelo's *The Sistine Chapel*. They are simply breathtaking. As we gaze upon such paintings and statues of Jesus and Mary, we might stop to reflect and pray, hoping to feel some of GOD's Presence and to experience blessing in our lives.

Let's consider for a moment the accuracy of the features in these artworks. Do we really know what Jesus looked like? There are similarities in each depiction. Have these features come after visions of Him? Perhaps. It is interesting to note, though, that different societies create Jesus in their own image. Jesus was in fact Jewish and most likely had dark skin, hair and eyes. Yet in the West he is often depicted with white skin and flowing golden-brown hair.

We seem to try to sculpt GOD into the shape of our own convenient beliefs. Do we limit Him by doing this? Is the level of the Presence that we receive limited by our own understanding of Who He is? He's bigger that that! The GOD Who created our universe, and beyond, can't be sculpted or shaped into what we choose. He won't be placed in a box and used when needed. We are the ones who need to be shaped into His mould, to become like Him.

When we receive Christ, it's as if He is presenting us with a luminescent candle. It's not something for us to carve or reshape as we desire. It will not fit into the receptacle of our own concepts of who He is. GOD is bigger than we know, and we must be open for Him to reveal His character to each of us. As we open up to Him, He will shape us and be revealed to us and in us.

Let's ponder this today and look for more of GOD. Statues and paintings remind of us of Him; however, our GOD doesn't live in these. Our GOD is invisible, yet His Spirit is all around us. So look for Him in spirit and in truth.

Father, help me to be submissive to You, the Master Sculptor. Please shape me into the Christ follower that you want me to become. Amen

27

Insignificant

> Therefore I tell you, don't be anxious for your life: what you will eat, or what you will drink; nor yet for your body, what you will wear. Isn't life more than food, and the body more than clothing? See the birds of the sky, that they don't sow, neither do they reap, nor gather into barns. Your heavenly Father feeds them. Aren't you of much more value than they?
> (Matthew 6:25–27)

Low self-esteem has always been a problem for me, having put up with put downs over the years. I was well prepared then for the sermon on this topic at my church one Sunday. Afterwards, I spoke to a pastor and decided to see her for counselling on the issue of feeling insignificant. While to me, it felt like a minor issue, it was bothering me.

At the end of our first meeting, the pastor wanted to pray for me while using her Jerusalem Oil. I almost said, 'Oh, don't waste that on me!', but managed to stop myself. I didn't want her to think that she wasn't helping me. She then began to pray, and at the end she asked me if I had heard from GOD and what He might have said to me. I didn't think there was anything, and then suddenly I blurted out 'Just!'

I explained that I'm not just a wife, a mum or a teacher aide. Jesus had died for me and now I am justified! Justified means I am important to Jesus. He loves me and has a purpose for me.

As I drove home, I chose to leave the car radio off, hoping that GOD would again speak to me. Soon I had to slow down because cars in front had stopped to allow a family of ducks to cross the road. There was a tall barricade on the other side, however, that the small family could not get over. Traffic was halted in both directions.

Suddenly, a man two cars in front of me got out of his car and started to shoo them to the edge. But the parents and four ducklings scattered in fright! At that point, quite unusually for me, I left my car, handbrake on and engine in idle, and went to assist him. Together, we got each duck, large and small, over the top of the barrier to freedom and safety. We waved to each other and then rushed back to our cars. As I drove away, I heard a whisper: 'You are more precious than any of these!'

I truly understood then my significance and that we are all precious to Him! Do you understand how significant you are to Jesus? If you don't know, then ask Him. I wonder how He'll show you. It could be in a most unexpected way. Our GOD is very creative.

Thank You, Father, for the compassion that You show me every day. You have such a personal touch. May I share that same compassion with those who I meet today. Amen

28

Implanted

> Therefore, putting away all filthiness and overflowing of wickedness, receive with humility the implanted word, which is able to save your souls. (James 1:21)

While wandering around my garden one day, I noticed something growing that was quite pretty, soft-looking and rather lacey. Still, in my mind it needed to come out. After all, it was a weed and certainly not welcome in my garden! I pulled at it, but it had a strong grip. So off I went to get my trusty 'weed puller' garden tool and began to dig.

Nothing! No result. I kept trying but after some more tugs and pushes without success, I chose to get the large garden fork. I dug much more deeply into the soil and discovered that this cute little plant had an enormous root! The root went straight down and was entangled with other roots nearby. This was becoming quite a big problem.

In the end, realising my own weakness against that plant's ability to grip the earth, I gave up and chose the path of 'bigger guns'. I would leave it to my husband's muscles to complete the task.

As usual for me, pondering this scenario reminded me of something – my own life and the entangled weeds of bitterness, resentment and unforgiveness within me. Not realising how deep that unseen root was in my garden was very much akin to my hidden hurts and grudges.

You see, a co-relation exists when we skim over such issues. We consider our personal stuff not to be a problem and leave things as they are. But others can see the problem even though we try to hide them. The unseen 'root' is enlarging and connecting to other 'roots' – resentments, complaints, disappointments – becoming more powerful and hard to conceal or remove. Roots of any kind tend to grow back and can be as large as the plant on top.

We must recognise Satan as the fertilizer of unforgiveness. Our loving Father promises to help if we cry out to Him. A nasty root of bitterness can be dissolved by the power of the Holy Spirit. Forgive, in His power, move on and praise Him, and like a bubble, POP! It's gone!

Have you ever had a nasty root problem like mine? Better remove that sucker.

Lord, I'm reaching out to You today. Help me to deal with my hurts and grudges. I forgive those who have wronged me and move on, in Jesus' name. Amen

29

The Chair

For as often as you eat this bread and drink this cup, you proclaim the Lord's death until he comes. Therefore whoever eats this bread or drinks the Lord's cup in a way unworthy of the Lord will be guilty of the body and the blood of the Lord. But let a man examine himself, and so let him eat of the bread, and drink of the cup. For he who eats and drinks in an unworthy way eats and drinks judgment to himself if he doesn't discern the Lord's body. (1 Corinthians 11: 26–29)

It was a beautiful Sunday morning. As was my custom, I dropped my two children off to Sunday School and went around to my mother's place to pick her up as we'd attend church together. As I drove into her street, I noticed a kerbside collection waiting to be picked up by the council. In that deposit of discarded rubbish an appealing piece of furniture caught my eye – a long reclining cane chair. Bingo!

On closer inspection I really liked it. I knocked on the door of 'Mrs Neighbour' who was happy for me to take it for free. I was pleased and explained that I needed assistance to move it, so I went for my mum's help. The lady said she was happy to wait for me.

On returning five minutes later, I was astonished to observe a man paying some money to 'Mr Neighbour' for that very chair. Mr and Mrs Neighbour had seemingly not spoken to each other about the agreement, and I had missed out. I was angry!

That Sunday, communion was offered at church. But I felt I couldn't partake in it because of the antagonism burning inside me against that man who had 'stolen' 'my chair'. I felt so ashamed. I knew that I had to be in a right relationship with GOD to share in communion with Him and I must resolve my feelings. So I chose to forgive him, through tears, even though he had done nothing wrong, and I let it rest. This act of forgiveness freed me.

A few weeks later, my children and I were returning from a birthday picnic at the beach. It was beginning to darken when they became thirsty. I remembered that we had some Pepsi in the boot, so I stopped and went to search in the esky for it. As I looked up, I saw the most unusual thing: an upturned cane chair stuck on a guidepost! Feeling flabbergasted and grateful, I got it off and fitted it into my small car just as it was, upturned, and drove home with it. GOD had organised it, even the best way it could fit in my car. I was astounded at His goodness and felt rewarded for my relinquishment of that previous chair, and my unforgiveness.

I still have this chair as it is a constant reminder of GOD's incredible goodness and kindness. His love and understanding never fail to amaze me, and I know it is for all of us who honour and obey Him. This is His very character. His kindness never ends. What a loving Father!

Have you a special memory of a gift given to you that holds special meaning?

 *Father, thank you for Your incredible gift of love for me day by day. Amen*

30

Terrible Loss

> I will rejoice in Jerusalem,
> and delight in my people;
> and the voice of weeping and the voice of crying
> will be heard in her no more. (Isaiah 65:19)

Sometimes, sad events occur in our lives unexpectedly. We are not prepared. These things happen to other people, not us! That's what I had thought too…

I had experienced those first kicks and I was longing for the arrival of this precious new baby who would be a playmate for its big sister. I was at the 21-week mark when my baby began to let his imminent arrival be known. My waters broke and I was immediately hospitalised. The baby was coming much too early because of a weakened cervix after a previous cancer operation. As he grew and became heavier, my body couldn't cope.

After four days in hospital with the end of my bed risen, and then four hours of labour, my baby came. He was stillborn and perfect in every way. He was so tiny, with hair and nails. He had the makings of an adorable child.

I believed that he was safe in the arms of Jesus. I took comfort in that confidence, dreaming of seeing him again one day. My perfect child was in a perfect place. That was great reassurance on one level, yet I was also feeling devastated. My friends and family were so supportive and tried their best to understand. But my loss was so personal and the pain excruciating. They were unable to empathise as they had not had this experience themselves.

On a Sunday, soon afterwards, I attended a communion service at my church. I raced out of the place in tears! It was the first time that I finally understood what it had cost Father GOD to give up His only Son to a cruel cross for my sins. The cost of losing my son was terribly confronting. How much more was the agonising pain for Father and Son. Somehow relating my pain to that of my Heavenly Father validated it and, over time, caused it to soften.

I take confidence that my son, who never got to take a breath, is alive forevermore with Jesus, my Conqueror. Praise His Name! I can't wait to meet them both in our eternal home.

Do you have someone in Heaven that you are longing to see?

Thank You, Father, that You understand my pain. When I lean on You, You comfort and lead me to a safe place where I can rest, restore and recover in Your arms. Amen

31

Sticks And Stones

> Death and life are in the power of the tongue; those who love it will eat its fruit. (Proverbs 18:21)

> A word fitly spoken is like apples of gold in settings of silver. (Proverbs 25:11)

'Sticks and stones can break my bones, but names can never hurt me.' Did your mum teach you that when you were a child? My mum did, but it didn't help when I was being bullied. Verbal insults can become our labels and we struggle with them. Criticism can endure for a lifetime as we get our sense of value from someone else. It can affect our psyche, emotions and character, even our plans and dreams.

Abuse can come in differing disguises, sometimes blatant and sometimes subtle. However hidden, it is powerful and controlling. At its worst, abuse is a criminal act against the innocent. But many of these people were victims themselves. Someone, somewhere in their past, has helped to create this nasty disposition in them by doing to them what they now do to others. It is a common pattern. *

Most of these individuals who abuse in any form usually have a low self-esteem and feel better about themselves when they put others down. This doesn't last and they continue to do it. By seeing that power as their weakness, you can take back your power by understanding that it is not your fault. You have not done anything wrong.

You have immense value as a daughter of the King of kings. GOD loves you so much that He sacrificed His only Son to rescue you from a hellish eternity. Now this gives you ultimate value! Don't believe the lies of abusers. Lies come from the 'father of lies', namely the devil. (John 8:44) Your Heavenly Father is not like that and sings words of truth over you. As you receive GOD's gift, you are saved and adopted into His family, becoming His daughter and precious to Him.

Are you feeling the love? By faith, allow His love to wash over you today. He is your Rescuer.

Father, I thank You for Your love and applause as You watch over me with Your approval. Amen

*Domestic violence or abuse of any kind is unacceptable, whether it's emotional, sexual or other – despite whatever has happened to the perpetrator in their past. Justice must prevail. If you're in need of a rescue from a situation, call out now. Help is available. Please refer to the Resources page at the back of this book.

32

PTSD

> Jesus therefore said to those Jews who had believed him, "If you remain in my word, then you are truly my disciples. You will know the truth, and the truth will make you free."
>
> They answered him, "We are Abraham's offspring, and have never been in bondage to anyone. How do you say, 'You will be made free'?"
>
> Jesus answered them, "Most certainly I tell you, everyone who commits sin is the bondservant of sin. A bondservant doesn't live in the house forever. A son remains forever. If therefore the Son makes you free, you will be free indeed. (John 8:31–36)

When we think of Post-Traumatic Stress Disorder, we immediately think of soldiers who've returned from war duties and have experienced incredible loss. Some have lost mates; some have lost limbs. Emotionally, they are hurting. Whatever the loss, it is accompanied by memories.

To deal with these memories, some soldiers immerse themselves into their war efforts by becoming professional soldiers for life. It is their career choice as they toughen up. But in a quiet moment, the painful memories and associated emotions return. These can be triggered by a car backfiring, a nightmare or a conversation. Instantly, they're returned to the source of the pain.

On a different scale, but just as real, terrible memories can haunt us too. Perhaps they come back as a particular word is spoken in conversation, and we are reminded of a car accident or domestic violence. These cataclysmic events are earth shattering in their effects and can lead to more violence, depression or even suicide.

There are many reasons for pain that's been inflicted upon us and the memories that are impossible to remove entirely from our brains. It's possible, however, to be free of the pain – through forgiving the offender. Forgiving may seem impossible at first. We may feel it is not what we want to do, and not what their actions deserve! But it is a necessary requirement for our ultimate healing.

Seek professional counselling as you need it, of course. But remember that GOD who forgave all our sins can help you to forgive whoever has hurt you. Forgiveness is the gift to ultimately set you free, and you deserve that gift! After all, GOD specialises in forgiveness. Ask Him to help you, and as reminders pop up, as they will, keep on forgiving and eventually you will be healed. It's all about you, and He's there waiting to help you. Who the Son sets free is free indeed!

Remember, forgiving those who hurt you doesn't mean in some cases that appropriate justice can't still be sought. But on that path, you can be free of unforgiveness, toxic anger and shame. Are you needing to reach out to Him today? He wants to touch and bless your heart.

Father, you know the pain that's inside me and you understand the justifiable hurts. So I'm asking you to please help me with forgiving those who have hurt me. Amen

It Rained Today

It rained today, pattering down,
Splashing in puddles all around.
I felt so teary, a little glum,
Remembering a past long undone

Then deep within me rose a commotion;
Soon I was rocked by waves of emotion
But skyward I looked as clouds were clearing;
Bright light burst through, a rainbow appearing

I knew GOD was speaking through that light;
"Come, my dear child, come out from that night
"Reach out to Me for I've always been here
"Let Me release you from those horrid fears
"Let Me teach you how to walk in My ways."
So I let GOD in and was full of praise!

He raised up a fountain from inside of me,
A spring of worship to Him eternally.
Now I know new hope from that vision that day;
I'll go on restored as I follow His way.
Sheryle Grace Wells

33

Grandma's Prayers

> We will not hide them from their children, telling to the generation to come the praises of Yahweh, his strength, and his wondrous deeds that he has done. (Psalm 78:4)

I am a city chick, having been born in a capital city, but there is a little bit of country inside me. My mother was a farmer's daughter. But because of drought, fires and hardship, she chose when she married to live in the city with her husband. She would often visit her parents on the farm with our family, and I loved those times.

My city life now is busy with everything I need close by. But when I leave my comfort to visit 'rurality', a new and different comfort and warmth comes over me. I love the animals, the fresh air and friendliness. Everything that I see, smell and feel is simply delightful.

These wonderful feelings take me right back to my childhood visits at my grandparent's farm. They were times of great joy and new discoveries. My grandad was always fun and had a great sense of humour. Both he and my grandmother had a strong faith. In fact, it was my grandma's prayers that led me to know Jesus as my personal Saviour.

Every night, before Grandma went to sleep, she knelt beside her bed and prayed for each family member. She faithfully prayed right up until the night before she left this life to meet Jesus Himself in Heaven. And I did indeed come to the Lord after she died. So, grandparents and parents, whoever you are, never stop praying for your loved ones. GOD even answers prayers after you are gone!

GOD's Word is filled with precious promises to bring back our family and friends from the land of the enemy. His love extends to everyone, no matter what they've done. So, pray for them! Plead in prayer for them to accept Jesus, as my grandma prayed for me. Stand in the gap: pray the prayers that they don't know they even need to pray. Pray on their behalf and claim them by faith in the Name of Jesus.! It's GOD's will because He doesn't want any one of us to perish. (2 Peter 3:9)

Did you have someone praying for you? Who will you pray for now? Who is first on your list?

Thank You, loving Lord, for the faithful prayers of someone special who led me into a relationship with You. Amen

34

Our Children

> Hear, Israel: Yahweh is our God. Yahweh is one. You shall love Yahweh your God with all your heart, with all your soul, and with all your might. These words, which I command you today, shall be on your heart; and you shall teach them diligently to your children, and shall talk of them when you sit in your house, and when you walk by the way, and when you lie down, and when you rise up. You shall bind them for a sign on your hand, and they shall be for frontlets between your eyes. You shall write them on the door posts of your house and on your gates. (Deuteronomy 6:4–9)

As parents, we instruct our children from an early age. We teach them to eat foods, to walk, to play and share, and to say 'please', 'thank you' and 'sorry'. We may take them to church as it's our job to 'train them in the way they should go'. We need to teach them how to know GOD. We also need to model the behaviour that we desire to see in them.

In the Bible, Jesus explained the meaning of the Parable of the Sower. The seed (GOD'S free salvation) was sown onto four different surfaces: (a) wayside (the devil stole it away); (b) the rocky soil (falls away during temptation); (c) thorny (choked out by selfish desires); and (d) the good ground.

All soils are to be encouraged to promote growth. Young children will grow as they watch and learn from our behaviour. Allow Jesus in us to be the model that they will see and choose to follow.

Remember, our children do not inherit salvation. GOD has no grandchildren, and each one of us needs to accept Him, like a little child. GOD is not Father to all of us, but He is Creator of all of us. It is only by acknowledging His Son's sacrifice on the cross for our sins, confessing our wrongdoings, and asking for forgiveness that we can be adopted by Father GOD and gain full access to Him. This is conversion. Our children need to respond in this way, as do we.

Have you talked with GOD about this, and with your children? It may be something to do today.

Lord GOD, I'm sorry for not preparing the soil as I should have when I was raising my children. May that rough, unprepared soil become fertile to receive Your message even now. Help them to see evidence and proof in my life, so they choose You for themselves. Amen

35

A Parent's Heart

> Hear, heavens,
> and listen, earth; for Yahweh[a] has spoken:
> "I have nourished and brought up children
> and they have rebelled against me.
> The ox knows his owner,
> and the donkey his master's crib;
> but Israel doesn't know.
> My people don't consider." (Isaiah 1:2–3)

I am proud to have been a mother to three children. GOD has blessed me. There have been difficult times as they were growing up. As well as health issues, my dearly loved children have been abused and experienced addictions, intense anxieties and deep depression. Each issue has caused lots of heartbreak. On this basis, I believe that I can write with some knowledge of anguish and heartache for parents.

These horrible events can shake anyone's world, from any family irrespective of education, social status or dysfunction. Let's face it: We all originate from a dysfunctional family. Even the first parents had to deal with jealousy and murder. The saying, 'Bad things happen to good people', applies more often than we realise and does not justify or help us in our time of grief.

But as Christians, we've been instructed to never stop trusting and believing because GOD has got this! He loves your family even more that you do, and He knows how you feel. GOD is doing something even when you don't see evidence of it. While you're waiting for that answer to your prayers, forgive yourself for any part that may have caused some pain. We are only human and do our best, but choices that others make are their own. Sometimes, it's nothing that you've done at all. You may have a rebellious, prodigal teenager stretching their wings. So stretch your wings of prayer and keep reminding yourself and believing that GOD has put Eternity in their hearts (Ecclesiastes 3:11).

Never stop praying. GOD's part in this is not over yet. He will do what He needs to do, and it's in His timing that things will happen. Simply trust, wait and believe. It will come to pass at the perfect time. Never, ever stop praying for GOD is collecting your prayers into a bowl. (Rev 5:8) When He answers your request, you will be able to say along with Mary, 'Blessed is she who believed, for there will be a fulfilment of the things which have been spoken to her from the Lord.' (Luke 1:45 WEB) Has He answered them yet? Stretch your faith and praise Him for the answer yet to come.

Lord, I give all my hopes and dreams to You because I know that they're safe with You. Thank You, in faith, for answers to prayer. I trust You for the outcome because now I expect it with confidence, in Your time. Amen

36

For A Hurting Friend

Blessed be the God and Father of our Lord Jesus Christ, the Father of mercies and God of all comfort; who comforts us in all our affliction, that we may be able to comfort those who are in any affliction, through the comfort with which we ourselves are comforted by God. For as the sufferings of Christ abound to us, even so our comfort also abounds through Christ. (2 Corinthians 1:3–5)

Believing that compassion without action is meaningless, I felt deep in my soul one day to write this letter to a dear friend. She was hurting from her teenage child's choices. It might be for you, or you may like to share it.

My dear friend

I feel compelled to write to you because I can feel your pain. Although I cannot identify with exactly what you are going through, I do understand what it's like when a child that you have raised with Christian ideals has not chosen to live by these. It seems that those values have been correctly instilled but sadly not chosen. And that young person seeks justification for their choices from their friends who they live and do life with.

I don't profess to comprehend or make judgements on anyone. But I do know that our Heavenly Father understands, and He will guide you lovingly through this difficult time.

Another thing I know is that even if children go off the track, it is important to walk with them on the journey. By doing this, the relationship remains open and the way back home always possible. The question is: What is the track? It can be different for each one of us. But GOD has already walked it and He has promised to be with us wherever we go.

One important fact to remember: Don't cast judgement. It is the job of the Holy Spirit to lead and guide them, and GOD has his own timing. Our job is to continue to love them and never stop praying, leaving it all up to Him. He loves your precious one more than you do. Let His love wash over you now too. Loving thoughts and prayers are sent to you.

Do you have a friend who might appreciate this letter? Consider sharing it with them. Are you hurt over the choices of someone close? I hope this letter comforts you too.

Father GOD, thank You for Your sustaining presence. You have always been with me. You have lovingly watched over me for my whole life. So now I am confident that I can trust You for the future of those I care about. I thank You, Lord. Amen

37

Big Arms

> Jesus called a little child to himself, and set him in the middle of them and said, "Most certainly I tell you, unless you turn and become as little children, you will in no way enter into the Kingdom of Heaven. Whoever therefore humbles himself as this little child is the greatest in the Kingdom of Heaven. Whoever receives one such little child in my name receives me. (Matthew 18: 2–5)

You may need to grab a tissue as you read this story, which my mother told me from her childhood. It's about her little brother who was two years younger than she.

When my grandmother was bathing two-year-old Bertie one night, she noticed a lump on his neck. She kept an eye on it and over time saw it was growing and not healing. So she took him to the town doctor. The result was a diagnosis of Hodgkin's Disease. Cancer!

My grandfather spent all the money he could find looking for a cure, trying every possible avenue. But in 1917, nothing much could be done to prevent the inevitable. The disease progressed rapidly, and after a mere six weeks, it was obvious that the end was closing in.

Towards the very end, Bertie wanted to sleep with his mother in her bed so that he'd get lots of cuddles in her arms. He wanted the 'big book' – the Bible – close to him. Not long before he died, he pushed his mother aside. Reaching up with his little hands, Bertie declared, 'I want to be in those big arms up there'. Shortly after this, he was quietly taken up into those big arms, to be embraced by Jesus. What a special time for my grandmother to be with her only son as he slipped gently into his eternity.

This has always been a story close to my heart as in it I see evidence of what is in store for all who love Him and are called by His name. We are called by His name when we become Christians, or Christ Ones. I am confident that when Jesus scoops me up in His time, I will meet not only Him but my uncle who never got to grow up.

This was a tragedy with a promise. How does this story resonate with you? Are you confident that Jesus is waiting for you with open arms?

Lord, thank You for reaching out to me with Your loving arms. What a wonderful promise I have of eternity spent with You and all of those who have gone before. Amen

38

Realising A Dream

> Behold, I tell you a mystery. We will not all sleep, but we will all be changed, in a moment, in the twinkling of an eye, at the last trumpet. For the trumpet will sound and the dead will be raised incorruptible, and we will be changed. (1 Corinthians 15: 51-52)

For a long time, I desired to go to Israel. So when an opportunity opened for me suddenly, I took it! I went on a tour with some special, Spirit-led, chosen-by-GOD women. Every day, we bonded together more closely as we walked, climbed and travelled by bus, discovering and experiencing new joys and wonders. Our tour, led by our knowledgeable tour guide, was an incredible experience. Never to be forgotten and always treasured.

We giggled, cried, prayed, ate many different delicacies and laughed hysterically together! We created an amazing, harmonious bond. That's how I understand that GOD Himself led each one of us to go on this wondrous journey.

Sadly, even wonderful events in our lives must come to an end. We all said our goodbyes with hugs, tears and promises to maintain contact with each other, which we still do. And then we began the l-o-n-g journey to our homes, first on the bus, then on two or three planes. It was exhausting. All I wanted to do was to get home and sleep in my own bed!

When I eventually arrived at my city, after one stopover where I slept little, I stayed awake all that day. I hoped I would then drop off and sleep soundly in my own bed that night. And sleep I did, but only for four hours or so. I woke up annoyed, but after a while, I began to doze and enjoyed the most beautiful dream. It left me feeling elated!

In this dream, I was awakened to the sound of my husband talking. He was up early preparing to depart for work. Upon investigating, I saw that he was chatting with seven of my travel buddies, including our tour guide. They had come to visit me because they couldn't sleep either! We all shared over hot chocolate. But then they had to leave in their car. I felt disappointed but also elated.

Upon awakening, I felt so joyful. What a beautiful dream that felt so real! I had a sense that a dream can happen in an instant, but Heaven is for eternity. So the fun times had only just begun! We will all share together again. Just like the call of a beautiful magpie piercing the crisp morning air, so too will be the Call of our Saviour to our Heavenly rest at His appointed time.

Dreams can be a little touch of GOD into our consciousness as we sleep. What dreams have you had? How about keeping a journal beside your bed to record when you awake any dreams that feel Spirit-led or insights.

Dear Father, my concept of forever has a beginning, middle and an end. But You are timeless, and everlasting is in Your Hands. Thank You, Lord. I trust You with my forever. Amen

39

You Are Invited

Let's rejoice and be exceedingly glad, and let's give the glory to him. For the wedding of the Lamb has come, and his wife has made herself ready." It was given to her that she would array herself in bright, pure, fine linen: for the fine linen is the righteous acts of the saints.

He said to me, "Write, 'Blessed are those who are invited to the wedding supper of the Lamb.'" He said to me, "These are true words of God." Revelation 19: 7–9

Have you ever been so hungry, so famished, that your food tasted delectable? Possibly after a diet or an illness or waiting in a fine restaurant. The meal was sumptuous and scrumptious, exceeding all your expectations.

That's a miniscule comparison of what it will be like at the Great Banquet, the Marriage Feast of the Lamb. The Lamb is Jesus Who voluntarily sacrificed Himself, dying in our place for our sins. At His table in Heaven, we will partake of the ultimate, unimaginable meal! We can't comprehend what that meal will consist of, but it will meet all our utmost desires and dreams. Jesus, the Lamb of GOD will be our Host.

Do you know if you have your reservation for a place at that table? It's totally free. The price has been fully paid for you. All you have to do to receive this invitation is to notify the Host. With honesty and humility, confess any wrong choices to Him. He will forgive you instantly, and then you'll have your invitation to attend.

Jesus is your Host, and He is the only way through which you can come to His table. You must personally approach Him. What a celebration it will be when the time has arrived! Are you getting hungry now? I can't wait to meet you and join with you in this feast. Encourage your friends to get their invitation too. There's room at the table and I'd love to meet them.

Have you been washed – cleansed, forgiven, saved – by the Blood of the Lamb?

Lord Jesus, I long to share with You in that feast, with all Christ Followers as we come together. Please reserve a place for me. Amen

40

Riding The Waves

> His mercy is for generations and generations on those who fear him. (Luke 1:50)

I had the most wonderful holiday at the beach a while ago. I was in the waves every single day. Now, I am not much of a swimmer, but I have a boogie board. This is a floating device that keeps me buoyant and allows me to travel along wondrous ocean waves. What exhilarating fun!

The waves were gleaming in the sunlight, constantly moving, never stopping. Feather-soft foam wriggled and writhed on the surface, making marvellous lacy patterns. These powerful movements of water were amazing to gaze at and to feel all around me. Their power moved me and carried me as I held on and rode. On some of these, I travelled all the way into the shore. It was such a brilliant feeling! On others, I chose to jump over, letting the refreshing sea spray splash over me.

I reflected on my Heavenly Father Who I felt was delighting in me as I enjoyed His magnificent creation. He was with me as I rode on the board. His promise is to be with me everywhere. He guided and directed each manoeuvre as we rode and glided together. I felt His presence with me, and I felt safe.

One day, I will leave this earth and travel to my Forever Home in Heaven. At times, I find myself pondering the Crystal Sea mentioned in the Book of Revelation. I wonder if there will be a little cove for me to play in.

Do you see our Father in the beauty of His creation? Take a moment to look around you today and simply enjoy His gifts. And don't forget to say thank you.

Heavenly Father, thank You for the times when I feel Your love as I enjoy Your creation. It's just a taste of what is to come, and I eagerly wait for that too. Amen

Salvation Prayer

Heavenly Father

I've strayed and I want to return to Your loving arms, once again. Please forgive me and accept me into Your everlasting kingdom. I believe in Jesus whose death on the cross paid my penalty and set me free, and I invite Him and the Holy Spirit into my life, completely. Thank you.

Amen

Resources And Help

Daily Bible Devotionals

- The Word for Today at Vision Christian Media www.vision.org.au
- DaySpring Daily Devotions www.dayspring.com

Online Bible And Study Tools

- Bible Gateway www.biblegateway.com

Mental Health Support

- Lifeline 131114 www.lifeline.org.au
- Beyond Blue 1300 22 4636 | www.beyondblue.org.au

Christian Counselling Services Australia

- Christian Counsellors Association (CCAA) http://www.ccaa.net.au

Abuse, Domestic Violence And Assault Help

- Emergencies: 000 (24/7)
- 1800 Respect National Helpline (White Ribbon Australia): 1800 737 732 www.1800respect.org.au
- DVConnect Womensline: 1800 811 811 (24/7)
- DV Connect Mensline: 1800 600 636 (9 am to midnight, 7 days)
- Kids Helpline: 1800 55 1800 (24/7)

- Men's Referral Service: 1300 766 491
- Lifeline Australia: 131 114 (24/7)
- Sexual Assault Helpline: 1800 010 120

For more information about a service in your state or local area download the DAISY App in your smartphone's App Store or Google Play.

Church Education On Domestic And Family Violence

- SAFER is an online tool that helps Australian churches understand, identity, and respond to domestic and family violence. www.saferresource.org.au

Alcohol And Drug Dependency Assistance

- Alcohol and Drug Information Service: 1800 177 833 (24/7)

All information above was correct at time of publication.

About The Author

Author Sherylle Grace Wells is a descriptive storyteller and observer of life who uses the power of story to inspire and encourage women through life's challenges. She draws on her many life lessons, hours personally studying GOD's Word, the Bible, and inspiration from the Holy Spirit. Her faith, strength and moral compass are grounded in her loving relationship with Jesus Christ. Sherylle is married to Robin and lives in a bayside suburb in Brisbane. She has three adult children and four grandchildren. A former teacher aide, she is now retired and enjoying her passion for writing, painting and walking along the beach with her dog.

www.ingramcontent.com/pod-product-compliance
Lightning Source LLC
Chambersburg PA
CBHW070524100426
42743CB00010B/1941